To Courtenay, who fi
a book: None of this would've happened with... y

To Susan, who makes my writing better by always telling me the truth, and to Michael, whose unwavering support gives me the strength to keep creating.

And to Elisa and Anna, who remind me that fighting for a better world is pretty bad-ass.

THE
LOCALIST

Think Independent,
Buy Local and Reclaim
the American Dream

Copyright © 2014 by Carrie Rollwagen
All rights reserved. No part of this publication may be reproduced,
distributed, or transmitted in any form or by any means, including
photocopying, recording, or other electronic or mechanical methods, without the prior written permission of the publisher, except
in the case of brief quotations embodied in critical reviews and
certain other noncommercial uses permitted by copyright law. For
permission requests, visit www.carrierollwagen.com.
Ordering Information:
Quantity sales. Special discounts are available on quantity
purchases by corporations, associations, and others. For details,
contact the publisher at the address above.
Orders by U.S. trade bookstores and wholesalers.
Please visit www.carrierollwagen.com.

The Localist: Think Independent, Buy Local and Reclaim the
American Dream / Carrie Rollwagen
ISBN 978-0-692-31948-2
ISBN 978-0-692-31949-9 (electronic)

1. The main category of the book —Biography & Autobiography
—Other category. 2. Business & Economics. 3. Small Business. I.
Rollwagen, Carrie. II. The Localist.

First Edition

18 17 16 15 14   1 2 3 4 5

The text type was set in Trade Gothic
The display type was set in Futura
Book design by Andrew Thomson
Cover design by Andrew Thomson
Ebook design by Jonathan Walls
Editing by Bobby Watson

TABLE OF CONTENTS

PREFACE: THROUGH THE RABBIT HOLE

A few years ago, I fell down a rabbit hole. Like Alice before me, I stumbled into a different world almost accidentally, and I found my worldview growing and shrinking … and shrinking more and growing all over again. When I started exploring what it means to buy local, I fell into a sort of Wonderland that spun me past new people, economic theory, different ways to think about money, and a new twist on patriotism. Everything I did changed: from drinking coffee to eating biscuits to taking walks. Like Alice, I got some wise counsel. Like her, I also met some weirdos.

This book is about small shopping, but it's also about my personal journey. I tried to write a book based on facts and figures, but they kept twisting themselves into doom and gloom. A book filled with pessimistic statistics wasn't one I wanted to write, and I doubt it's one you want to read, so what follows is more story than stats, more philosophy than flowcharts. This book certainly has a strong foundation of fact, but it's told through the prism of my own story and adventures in local shopping.

Sometimes this means connecting a big concept about macro-economics to a random story from my child-

Do you want the job done right or do you want it done fast?

— Homer

Well like all Americans — fast!

— Marge
The Simpsons

CHAPTER ONE

****

CORPORATIONS, A LOVE STORY:

How Big Companies Won
Our Hearts with Service,
Speed and Savings

****

WE HEART CORPORATIONS

Let's get this out of the way at the beginning: I'm not here to shame anybody. I've been pretty committed to shopping locally for about four years. I'm writing a book about it. That means America's small shops are important to me, but it doesn't mean I think they're perfect or that corporations are always bad. I like to save money and time as much as anybody else, and I don't think that's a bad thing.

I don't shop at Wal-Mart, but that doesn't mean I'm not tempted by those smiley-face-emblazoned falling prices. I'm not particularly lazy or selfish (maybe that's debatable), but I love walking into a mall, feeling the rush of the air-conditioned and perfumed air, and thinking the answer to my problems just might be at the other end of a credit card swipe. It feels like Target, Anthropologie and Whole Foods really "get" me, and shopping there makes me feel happy. Maybe that feeling is shallow, but sometimes a temporary thrill is better than nothing.

Enjoying the benefits of big box shopping isn't anything to feel guilty about; those reasons we hear for shopping locally — "mom-and-pops are nicer, small shops have better service, we miss the good old days

of Main Street and Mayberry" — don't even turn out
to be true much of the time. We aren't Mayberry, but
we shouldn't be (our world isn't perfect, but America is
at least less overtly racist and misogynistic than it was
when Sheriff Andy was in charge). We love convenience,
and we love saving money. We like that corporations can
make us feel included and special. Are there reasons to
choose independents over corporations? Spoiler alert: I
think there are. But the idea that small shops are heroic
and corporations are evil isn't one of those reasons.

We hear a lot of rhetoric saying that local shops are
more authentic than big box stores, but what does that
even mean? If corporations are better at giving us what
we want, maybe that actually makes them more authentic than the indies. The world has changed: Technology
has made speed not only a possibility but an expectation.
A recession has left us with less expendable income. We
like the way big box stores echo these changes: It's nice
to be able to pull off the interstate at any given Burger
King and know exactly what to order and where to pee.
It's predictable. It's comfortable. It's kind of impersonal
(even most "personal" service in big box stores is scripted), but sometimes that's exactly what we're looking for.
We're so unused to making conversation with strangers,
to giving up our personal space and our personal time
for someone else, that it's become a difficult thing to

do. And we don't want to make that kind of sacrifice just to get a quick hamburger (or fifty quick hamburgers, if we're shopping from Costco). Connection is uncomfortable, and corporations don't force us to connect through anything but our debit cards and (maybe our smartphones). We are known, not by our names, but by our customer numbers. Yes, that corporate model can be anonymous and monotonous, but sometimes monotony is comforting. While it's true that the big boxes can be soulless, that doesn't mean they have to be or that they always are.

Why do we pass up independently owned shops in favor of their corporate counterparts? One common explanation is that we just don't understand what they have to offer. (Personal service is the big talking point here.) Yes, independents have personal service, but maybe that's not what we're looking for anymore. Maybe the efficiency and affordability of big box stores is what we want, and not what we settle for. It could be that the personal touch we're supposed to be missing is the very thing we're avoiding.

The idea that many "good ol' days" proponents teach — that Americans are lazy and selfish, and that liberals or conservatives or young people or rap music or Miley Cyrus or whatever the punching-bag-of-the-week happens to be — have ruined our country is too simplistic to be true. It's also hypocritical — I'm willing to bet most of us like Wal-Mart, at least on some level, even if we don't want to admit it. (At least, I know that I do.) Besides being reductive and judgmental, this idea is also counter-productive: Guilt might make us feel bad, but it won't change our buying patterns.

As a nation, we shop differently than we used to, but that's because our world is different. From small shops to big businesses, from our local economies to the global economy, from Mars to our backyards, our lives have changed, and our ideas about small business haven't caught up with that. We might feel a pang of guilt when we see yet another "going out of business" sign in the window of a local shop, but we still don't stop, because our guilt about not shopping small is mostly nostalgia — that memory of Mayberry with its soda shops and friendly community chats. But our culture has changed, and we don't walk whistling through the streets anymore, lazily swinging fishing poles over our shoulders. We're driving. We're busy. Why slowly sip a milkshake before heading to a fishing hole when you can get a McFlurry and a Filet-O-Fish from McDonald's in a fraction of the time? We usually don't know our neighbors, much less our grocers and bankers and baristas.

I may prioritize neighborhood shopping, but I like speed, dependability, affordability and anonymity as much as the next American. I like going into a store and knowing everything will probably be just where I want it to be, and that every employee will be helpful and (relatively) kind without asking the same from me in return. Is that selfish? Well, yeah. But our modern attitude isn't necessarily bad (well, the not knowing our neighbors bit is probably bad). It's a response to how incredibly busy our lives have become, how stressed we feel, and how each one of us is constantly pulled in so many different directions by obligation and responsibility. After a long day chasing the elusive end of our to-do lists, the last thing we want to give time and attention to is getting dinner, running errands and going shopping, so it's easier to choose a store where we can do everything all at once.

We have a vague idea that small shops are charming, that somehow small business is the backbone of the economy: that we *SHOULD* be shopping at mom-and-pop stores. But if that nagging feeling doesn't have facts supporting it, it's not a basis for true conviction or change. Remember Jiminy Cricket from Pinocchio? He was a singing bug with a waistcoat, and he tried to get his puppet buddy to stop lying by listening to his conscience and doing what was right. Jiminy Cricket was tiny, a little bit shrill and, well, a bug. He didn't inspire change that was deep, ethical and truly right. Most of our conviction about small shopping is based on antiquated ideas and is too much like our cricket friend — silly, small, and easily tuned out.

BEWARE THE INDEPENDENT: SHOPKEEPERS ARE CREEPY

Too often, when local shop owners ask us to shop with them, they try to play the pity card: "Buy from us, we're nice and quirky and we barely stand a chance!" They're like that nerdy dude in the bar who tries to pick you up by doing magic tricks — he definitely doesn't have what you want, but when you try to blow him off, he looks like he might cry. Plenty of people feel sorry for that guy, but nobody goes home with him; and nobody shops local out of pity either.

There's a great TV show called Portlandia that lovingly mocks Portland, a city that's become a mecca for young hipsters trying to lead more "authentic" lives. It seems like every wannabe musician or wannabe librarian or wannabe organic farmer decides to live in Portland, and the show lovingly mocks their aesthetic. As Portlandia skewers the sacred cows of hipsterdom, local businesses do not escape: The shopkeepers of Portlandia are out of touch with customers, offering ridiculous, incredibly specific merchandise. They slap woodland creatures onto any and every item in the shop and call it art. They follow customers around their stores, harassing them as they browse, guilt-tripping them into buying things they don't want, and declaring the items they do want unavailable.

These shopkeepers are caricatures, but we recognize them because that's how lots of local business owners behave. You know the feeling — you walk into a locally owned shop and feel the owner's eyes the whole time. You feel the desperation in their stares. You don't understand how the shop is still in business in the first place, because their stock is low and their store is shabby and they have no grasp on public relations or social media or even basic social graces. The shop looks more like someone's living room than a store, and you can't find anything without help from the quirky owner. You don't want to stay, but you don't feel like you can leave without talking to the owner (who looks like he might cry if you leave empty-handed), so you pray for a distraction: Maybe the phone will ring, or the tabby cat that's inexplicably sitting on the counter will leap onto the cash register, or the owner will get so absorbed in his issue of *Cat Fancy* that you can dart out the door before he notices you're moving.

Maybe there are customers who like this feeling, but

the majority of us just feel creeped out. We don't want to feel like the financial and emotional health of the owner is in our hands. We don't want to feel watched while we're shopping. We don't want to make a trip across town just to find empty shelves. Sometimes all we really want is to head to Wal-Mart, where we know what we want will be stocked fifty-deep on the shelves and no one will bother us. What we want is freedom not to buy and to be free of obligation.

I don't always like walking into a locally owned shop and feeling like I have to chat with the shop owners; I like walking into a store and feeling anonymous. When I go into Target (or Barnes and Noble, or Best Buy, or wherever), it's all about me: The temperature is perfect, the store is organized and laid out so everything I want is at my fingertips, and the staff is trained to help me when I need them and ignore me when I don't. That song in Cheers says, "Sometimes you want to go where everybody knows your name." But I usually want to go where no one does.

WE'RE ALL BEAUTIFUL SNOWFLAKES (WITH CUSTOM COFFEE ORDERS)

We like to be anonymous when we choose to be, but we also want to feel special and important. Is that a contradiction? Sure, but we're human beings, and we're complicated, so we're allowed to have contradictory feelings. The truth is that we want our unique needs met, but we don't want to feel the heavy weight of responsibility either. Creating a shop that makes us feel special without asking anything from us in return is tough; finding that balance is difficult, and independent stores often get it wrong. They give us too much attention while big boxes have mastered the art of getting just close enough to make us feel important without really invading our personal space.

Big box stores have done an outstanding job of combining advertising, in-store messaging, and social media messaging to give products stories that we can easily take on as our own. We like the attention, but we also like it because it's not *TOO* much attention. In our society real connection feels weird. We usually move far away from our families, and even when we're close, we communicate with them through screens. We rarely know our neighbors at more than a small-talk level. At work, we're not encouraged to discuss family, politics, religion, or anything truly important.

That's why, even when the local store experience is genuinely better, sometimes we'd rather shop at the big box anyway, because we crave that emotional distance. At Starbucks, the barista might write my name on a cup, and I might feel defined by a doppio espresso, but that's as far as our relationship goes. That kind of definition is necessarily shallow — but it's also easy and comfortable. The writer Nora Ephron describes this perfectly in her movie *YOU'VE GOT MAIL*. Ephron, a kindred spirit of mine (at least when it comes to coffee and books), often sneaks little essays into her screenplays, and here's a great one from the movie:

"The whole purpose of places like Starbucks is for people with no decision-making ability whatsoever to make six decisions just to buy one cup of coffee. Short, tall, light, dark, caf, decaf, low-fat, non-fat, etc. So people who don't know what the hell they're doing or who on earth they are can, for only $2.95, get not just a cup of coffee but an absolutely defining sense of self: Tall! Decaf! Cappuccino!"

We laugh, but we all enjoy the self-definition that big

boxes provide. Our clothes, our music tastes, our books, and, yes, our Starbucks orders, all serve as signposts to the world, announcing the people we are (or maybe the people we want to be). Through advertising, big boxes assign character to certain products, and when we buy them, we get to feel like we're taking on that character for ourselves.

Nora Ephron is right — coffee orders are a great example of this. Order a soy latte, and you're telling everyone that you're health-conscious, maybe a vegetarian, and that you care about the planet. Order a sugar-free, non-fat vanilla latte, and you're telling us that you place a high premium on looking good and watching your weight. Ask for a white mocha with extra whip and caramel drizzle, and you're saying the opposite (also maybe that you've had a bad day). Of course, these definitions might not be true at all. You could order soy because you're lactose intolerant, sugar-free because you're diabetic, extra sugar because you're an eight-year-old boy. The point is, these are values that corporations assign to the drinks, and their social associations are as much of a selling point as their taste.

My favorite example of this is the Starbucks Caramel Macchiato. The ingredients of this drink are almost identical to those of a vanilla latte, and the drink bears no resemblance to a traditional macchiato (espresso shots marked with foam). Really, the Caramel Macchiato is neither caramel nor a macchiato, but that's not the point. The drink is successful because it's fun to order, and it lets you take on the character of a coffee snob. To love real macchiato, you'll need to cultivate a taste for espresso. To love a Caramel Macchiato, all you really need to enjoy are milk, sugar and fancy words.

When we shop locally, we're forced to acknowledge the people who run the shops as actual human beings. We have to look them in the eyes. The words they say to us aren't corporately scripted. We have to admit that the way we treat people and the way we spend our money makes a difference, and we've become such an insulated culture that we're actually uncomfortable when faced with real human contact. Sometimes when people are nice to us, we see it as strange, even when they're just being kind. It's tough to talk with people face-to-face when so much of our communication happens through our phones or computers. The very thing small shops think they have going for them — the personal touch — might be exactly what's keeping us away.

YOU'VE GOT MAIL is a Meg Ryan/Tom Hanks vehicle that manages to be sweet, charming, and a love letter both to the idea of romance and to the city of New York. I liked the movie as much as the next bookish girl (even though it condones emotional cheating and sort of implies that a woman needs a man's help to run a business). The heroine is a shop owner who cares about character, literature and uniqueness. She's a champion of the things many of us say we love about small-town America (even though her small town is a big city). Her customers and her authors claim to stand with her, but in the end, they spend their money at the discount chain, and the independent goes out of business. YOU'VE GOT MAIL is a saccharine-sweet story that makes true love seem believable and the collapse of small shops seem inevitable. Its message is that the little guy loses, and that's an unhappy ending that seems to be coming true.

LET'S GET TOGETHER

If you spend a lot of time in coffee shops — and I do — you'll see people go to great lengths to make themselves at home in a public place. I watched a guy set up his huge home printer on a café table and proceed to print multiple copies of his resume. I've seen people take off their shoes and socks (socks!!) to get more comfortable while studying in public. I've watched multiple people unpack complete picnics onto the tables at bookstores without buying any books or coffee, and I've seen couples go past PDA to full-on making out where customers were ordering cappuccinos.

A lot of the most successful stores aren't simply places to go and buy stuff. They're more than that. They make us so comfortable that we almost feel like we're at home. Just like ordering a certain drink is an easy way to establish a personality, making ourselves cozy in big box stores has become a way of holding onto the idea of community and neighborhoods without really having to get to know anybody.

The writer Ray Oldenburg coined the term "third place" to describe the phenomenon of community gathering places. His basic idea is this: As modern humans, we go to work, and we go home. But we feel best when we have another place, a third place, where we can also feel comfortable and be social. Formerly, this was often a barbershop, small café, or a neighbor's front porch. Now, it's places like Starbucks and Barnes and Noble. Of course, big box stores certainly don't have the market cornered on customer service or feeling like a third place, but small shops no longer have exclusive rights to personal service and an experience that feels authentic. Corporations may not be able to perfectly duplicate the magic of the mom-and-pop, but that hasn't stopped them from trying hard. And some of them are getting pretty close.

THE LOCALIST

I feel welcomed and at home at my "local" Barnes and Noble. I'm a book lover, so I have a natural affinity for the place. But for many years, they also designed the store to encourage loitering, something lots of retail businesses actively discourage. Barnes and Noble felt like a huge library that allowed you to get lost inside and find your own charming corner. Sure, you could gather in the café with friends. But you could also find a comfortable armchair large enough to curl up in and read books and magazines for free. They put portraits of famous writers around the store and especially in the café, giving the impression that you were sharing your coffee with Virginia Wolfe and Ernest Hemingway. Even now, when most of Barnes and Nobles' armchairs have been replaced with racks of Legos and some of the books have been swapped for ereader islands, Barnes and Noble feels a little like home to me.

It's not just the comfy chairs that make us feel at home in corporate stores. Many chains also put emphasis on customer service, creating lively scripts for their employees to learn and riff off of, and make sure to put lots of information in the hands of their staffs so customers can get help whenever and with whatever. In some cases, the service at big box stores is now better than the service at indies. Their prepared scripts can't help every time, but they can help most of the time, and that positive experience is what we remember. Big box companies also have a lot of money to throw at the customer service problem. If you're deliberating on an item at Whole Foods, an employee can open it up and let you taste it for free. If you order shoes from Zappo's, you'll get incredibly quick delivery and free shipping on returns. And if you complain that your Starbucks Caramel Macchiato is too cold, your barista will not only make you a new one immediately, but she'll give you a coupon for a free drink next time you visit. These companies have grown so big, and their profits are so huge, that they can afford to treat us like royalty, and that service keeps us coming back.

If big boxes already feel like home, it's not a stretch to say the companies they represent feel like friends (or even family). With social media, we can now hear from our corporate-BFFs every day, and we can talk back to them, too. When we have bad service, we get on Twitter and let the company know they've hurt us. When we find a good deal, we put it on Instagram and advertise for the company to our own followers. Most big companies have some sort of social media presence, and the good ones have teams ready to respond back immediately, thanking us when we support them and tweeting back apologies, coupons, and offers to fix our problems when we complain.

Starbucks in particular has worked hard to become a

"friendly" company, reaching out to customers through their baristas as well as through social media channels. They've succeeded in becoming a third place in many neighborhoods. At a Starbucks, you can sit in a comfortable chair or choose a table with plenty of space to spread out. You can chat with people at the next table or be by yourself, get a drink from a barista who knows your order, pick up a newspaper or even a book. You can get lost in conversation, work or relaxation. You can sit for hours with your laptop or grab a quick latte before you run to work. It's welcoming and familiar. It may not be true that everybody knows your name, but the barista probably does. And if she doesn't, she'll find out, because it's written on your cup.

IT'S NOT YOU; IT'S ME: WHERE'S THE CORPORATION WE FELL IN LOVE WITH?

As tempting as it is to think corporations are our friends, it isn't really true. The corporate world is ultimately set up to please the shareholder, not the consumer. Big box stores seem friendly not because they actually like us, but because they get more money out of us that way. Maybe that's okay — we're using each other, and we both get what we want out of the relationship. Or maybe our relationship is dysfunctional and a lot more destructive than we think. It's worth looking past the surface to discover what really happens when we buy from big box stores and to examine whether or not they're actually making us happy. Think of it as marriage counseling between us and corporations: Maybe we'll be even happier in our buying decisions than we were before; maybe we'll break up. Corporations want us to believe they offer such unbelievable savings and speed because they're nice, or because they're magic. As logical people, we know neither one is really true. It's important to find out what exactly we're sacrificing for convenience and to think about whether or not what we're giving up is worth losing.

Before we toss our small shops overboard in favor of discounts and free shipping, it's smart to look at where those discounts are coming from, at what corporations are actually giving us in return for our loyalty, and at what the world without independent stores — the world we're creating — will really be like. Each of our purchases starts a domino effect, changing not only our personal lives but also our local and national economies. Each credit card swipe effects me; it also effects my neighbors and my community and the fast food workers and baristas that I barely know. For a culture that loves isolation as much as we do, that thinking can be difficult. It's also important.

Big box shopping seems infinitely more convenient because it seems to save us time and money. Those are the resources we're always running short on, and it's nice to think we're getting them back when we buy online or from a huge retailer. The trouble is, that might be an illusion. We're not saving as much money as we'd think because we're buying more stuff instead of putting our savings in the bank. And time? Well, time can't be stockpiled. The hours we save getting all our stuff at a chain store gets channeled back into an ever-growing list of errands (that happen to require more shopping trips) and more mindless entertainment (using technology that we also have to pay for).

Some people say time is money. I'm not sure this translates if you spend an entire day binge watching Cake Wars, but I get their point. Time and money are important to us as Americans — never more so than now, when we've been going through a tough recession and we try to pack a lot (including, sometimes, second jobs) into our days. We are a busy people, and we are an upwardly mobile people. Our needs for more hours in the day and more money in our wallets are two big reasons we don't shop small, because buying locally seems time-consuming and expensive.

The technological revolution that gave us smart-phones and laptops has changed our expectations about waiting. When it comes to streaming a video or down-loading a file, it's seconds, not minutes or hours, that mean the difference between fast and slow — we've been taught by our phones and our computers to expect things to come quickly. Speed is at a premium in our lives, and that has an impact on shopping. Why go to a record store to buy music when we can immediate-ly download songs from iTunes? Why visit a bookstore when there's a whole library on the Kindle? Corporate stores have tools like lightning-fast operating systems and nationalized shipping services at-the-ready to help them compete in a world that prioritizes speed, but most small shops do not. Their shelves aren't packed as full as big box shelves are, and we no longer have the patience to wait for an item that isn't in stock. How do indepen-dents with limited shelf space and limited buying power compete with the warehouse that is a Best Buy store? In most cases, they don't.

A store like Wal-Mart or Target stocks a little bit of everything, so we can be reasonably sure they'll have what we're looking for. Want to pick an end table while restocking the dish soap? Aisle fourteen. Want to grab a frozen dinner while getting supplies for a school project that's due tomorrow? No problem. Need some luggage *AND* a handgun? In no time at all, you'll be all set for packing — and you'll be packing.

Saving trips usually saves time, and it also cuts down on the stress of having to plan an agenda for errands. Especially for poor families, single parents, or families with parents working two or more jobs, the convenience of having everything in one place can be extraordinary. Seeking out unfamiliar, locally owned stores can be an adventure. But who has time for adventure?

HOLLY JOLLY PROFIT MARGINS

Besides the time, there's money. Item-by-item, shopping locally costs more. Sometimes the differences are small, and sometimes they're dramatic: like when we contrast local, organic lettuce with that trucked into a superstore. The higher quality merchandise that some independents carry explains some of the price difference, but plenty of indies carry the same products as their big box rivals, and the prices at the smaller shops are still higher. Independent bookstores, for example, have the exact same books as Amazon, but they charge a lot more. Big box products tend to cost less per item even before we've factored in savings from rewards programs, discounts, and free shipping.

Why can corporations offer us these awesome prices? Behind the glass of company skyscrapers, are CEOs acting as corporate Santas, jolly old elves handing out discounts for the pure joy of giving? I won't pretend to know what CEOs do behind closed doors (although I do enjoy the image of a company president walking through the halls sucking candy canes and wrapping up confer-ence calls with a hearty "ho-ho-ho"), but I do know that companies want us to spend more, not less. Big box stores want us to think it is economies of scale (their ability to buy and ship in bulk) and corporate efficiencies that make their products cheaper, but that's only partly true. Those things do have an impact, but mostly big box stores make things cheaper because low prices get us to spend a lot more money.

Sometimes corporations do a kind of bait-and-switch, where they lower prices on some items just to hike up the prices of others. If we're drawn in with savings, we usually don't notice that the other items we're buying are more expensive than usual — CEO Santa gives out free hot chocolate so we don't notice that he's jacked up the price on Jack-in-the-Box. The bait-and-switch model is also at play when a company lowers their prices to drive a competitor out of business and then raises them again when the competitor is gone. This tricky little swap isn't unusual, but the main reason corporations discount doesn't involve such a complex switcheroo. Usually, big boxes make things cheaper simply because we'll supplement the money we "save" by making impulse purchases anyway. We spend more and they make more in the long run.

We all think we don't do this, and we all do it — if we didn't, the discount model wouldn't work and corporate stores wouldn't use it. You know the situation: You go to Best Buy on Black Friday for an unbelievable deal on a Blu-ray player. Maybe you save $50; then you buy two Blu-ray movies, because obviously you'll want something to watch. On the way to check out, you pass a spinner of iPhone cases and decide to pick up a couple of them for stocking stuffers, and in the check-out aisle you treat yourself to a pack of gum and a Coke, and then you buy the store's insurance on the player (just to be safe). So you walk out spending more than the sticker price of the Blu-ray before the discount. It's very true that you got more for your money. But you also spent more money. That's an important distinction, and it's how big box stores make a profit, by manipulating us with their smartly designed aisles and checkout kiosks, perfectly positioned to push impulse buying.

The natural extension of the impulse-buy model is a sort of subscription model, where a corporation sells a device at or below cost so you'll use it to make more purchases from the company. Apple knows that if we buy iPads and iPhones, they've got us on the line for music and movies. Amazon's Kindle takes this a step farther, locking Kindle's system so users actually *CAN'T* buy books from any other company. This kind of restrictive technology means lower prices, but it also means less innovation, more corporate control and fewer customer choices.

This isn't how our grandparents shopped. They didn't impulse-buy nails when looking for a hammer at the hardware store, and they didn't grab a few extra spindles of thread in the checkout line at the fabric store unless they were actually running low on thread. But we do many things differently than our grandparents did, and that isn't always bad. (For example, my grandpa likes to drink cabbage juice that's drained off the sauerkraut and suck the marrow out of bones, and I prefer a latte and a nice muffin.) The trouble isn't that times have changed; it's that the quality of what's available has changed too — these aren't our grandparents' products. The toasters and record players and even the clothes made half a century ago are still functioning today, but the ones we bought at Wal-Mart last year are already broken or falling apart. This hasn't happened because manufacturers forgot how to make functional products. It's happened because corporations now refuse to pay for quality.

Say you're buying headphones. You find the make and model you want, and you search online for the lowest price. You think you're getting the same headphones either way, so you might as well buy discount, right? Today those headphones are the same. Tomorrow they won't be. To get those prices so low, big box stores strong-arm and undercut their suppliers, forcing artificially cheap products out of them. To survive, those companies have to find ways to somehow make their products more cheaply, and there are two common ways to do that: Cut labor costs by mistreating workers (since magic elves aren't yet an available source of free labor) or cut the quality by using shoddy materials and cutting corners (or both). Corporate stores tell us it's reasonable to expect high quality at dirt-cheap prices, but even common sense tells us that's not true. This is why all our stuff is broken. This is why we can't have nice things. It's because we insist on low prices, and our cheaply made products fall apart. And that's why, if you want a toaster that stands the test of time, you'd better buy one that's already fifty years old.

CARRIE ROLLWAGEN

WHEN THEY WERE GOOD, THEY WERE VERY, VERY GOOD

When I was in kindergarten, we performed a play that was mostly made up of nursery rhymes. I remember Little Jack Horner sitting in a corner (that kid was lucky because he didn't have lines and got to sit on a stool the whole play), a boy who stuck his thumb in a pie and pulled out a plum (the plum was played by a purple balloon attached to his finger — this was the eighties, and choking hazards weren't such a big deal), and me as Little Bo Peep. (Although, given my stubbornness, "Carrie, Carrie, Quite Contrary" might've been more appropriate.) Those nursery rhymes really stuck in my head; especially this one: "There once was a girl who had a little curl, right in the middle of her forehead. When she was good, she was very, very good ... and when she was bad, she was horrid."

When corporations are good, they can be very, very good. Big box doesn't necessarily equal bad, and corporations aren't inherently evil. Corporations can take actions that benefit their communities and the country. But the truth is, they usually don't. Big businesses doing good things on a regular basis, not just when they're in trouble and need a public relations boost, are rare.

38

THE LOCALIST

Most of the time the company acts in the interest of its shareholders, not its people — not its employees and not even its customers.

When corporations enact positive changes, they have a powerful effect. Although red tape and shareholder logistics can slow policy changes at huge companies, their sheer size and scale mean that, when good changes come, they have an incredibly big impact. That can be for the betterment of society. If changes at independent shops are small waves lapping the shore and changing the landscape over time, changes from corporations come like tidal waves. Sometimes that sea change is just what we need, but sometimes it's destructive. It's up to us to be informed enough to tell the difference.

When corporations do good, their changes spread quickly and widely. McDonald's gets a lot of (deserved) criticism for the quality of their food and their apparent lack of care for employees. But in the book *FAST FOOD NATION*, Eric Schlosser writes that when McDonald's made changes to bring (marginally) healthier beef into its restaurants, the entire industry reformed. Because it takes a lot of cows to meet America's taste for Big Macs, McDonald's is a huge beef buyer, and almost every big producer relies on them for business. When McDonald's changed their standards, the factory farms had to change or lose their biggest customer. They raised better beef, and all burger buyers, not just McDonald's, benefitted. McDonald's got what they wanted not just because they have a scary clown on their side (although that probably didn't hurt), but because they have massive buying power, and that buying power can be used for good. This kind of change could benefit us globally by creating a market for sustainably harvested produce and factories that are more responsible with their carbon footprints. Environmental groups haven't met much success with regulating industries that pollute, especially in developing countries. But when big corporations refuse to purchase products from polluters, or they change the standards on the food they buy to encourage better farming practices, the market can change a lot more quickly than it does from political intervention and regulation. Changes in corporate buying could quite literally give us a better world.

Other companies do good by taking care of their staffs. Starbucks and Whole Foods offer insurance (including vision and dental) to their employees, even when they work as few as 20 hours a week. (I worked for Starbucks as a part-time barista, and I had better insurance than I did as a full-time writer for Time Warner.) In practice, this functions as a kind of insurance for artists, and it's why you'll often find photographers, graphic designers, writers and other artists with non-standard careers that don't provide insurance serving your cappuccino at Starbucks or stacking avocados at Whole Foods.

Insurance for part-time employees isn't required by law, and while corporations like Wal-Mart tried to avoid paying insurance even for people who basically worked full-time (by scheduling them just shy of the 40-hour mark), companies like Whole Foods and Starbucks stepped up and provided a benefit that wasn't required of them. Maybe if more corporations had followed suit (and if Congress looked for a capitalistic solution instead of ignoring the problem), Obamacare, the Affordable Health Care Act that has so divided Congress and the country, might not have been necessary in the first place. We all win when companies like Starbucks and Whole Foods prioritize health care for their staffs, because then their employees don't become a drain on the budgets of emergency rooms and subsidized health care the way most Wal-Mart (and other part-time) employees do.

When CEOs make decisions that benefit their employees or their consumers or their cattle, we all benefit. There's even monetary incentive to do good things, because warm-and-fuzzy business practices attract customers, and then those customers spend money, and then profits go up, and then the company does more good (cue that Lion King "Circle of Life" song). In theory that makes sense, and sometimes it works. The trouble is, it often doesn't work. Our corporate system is so convoluted, with parent companies gobbling up smaller businesses into huge conglomerates, that it doesn't always function the way it's supposed to. Most people don't know, for example, that GAP, Banana Republic and Old Navy are the same company ... or that Amazon owns Zappo's and Audible and IMDb and Goodreads ... or that Kraft owns Cheez Whiz *AND* Velveeta *AND* Easy Mac. The leaders of these companies are smart enough to realize that, in many cases, the public won't know or care when they do bad things, because they're done in the shadows. Even the good things they do happen only when we're looking. And how often are we really looking?

The corporate drive to do good often falters when their actions don't positively change sales. When it seemed like consumers wanted environmentally sustainable products, the "green" movement had massive customer support, and companies scrambled to try to find sustainable products and recycled packaging. But when the sales numbers didn't jump, many companies stopped trying to actually change their business practices. The sad news is, corporate "good" is often just window dressing, and when we manage to peek through the curtains, the real picture isn't pretty.

Small shops are the underdogs of our economy, and it isn't fun to root for the underdog. In the movies, sure

— but that's because we're pretty sure the little guy's going to win in the end, or there wouldn't be a movie about him. In reality, unless we think David really stands a chance, we usually side with Goliath, and for good reason: Odds are, the giant's going to win the day, and giants don't have a reputation for being gentle with the people who bet against them. But there are plenty of reasons to join this fight anyway. America's corporations aren't meeting our needs the way we think they are, and the cost of their speed and discounts is just too high. Our independent shops are still worth fighting for. After all, sometimes the underdog does win, and the victory that seemed improbable is that much sweeter in the end.

I wish there was a way to know you're in the good old days before you've actually left them.

—Andy Bernard
The Office

CHAPTER TWO

****

THE GREAT
WAL-MART FAST:

My Year without
Big Box Shopping

****

RESOLUTION FEVER: I'M ADDICTED TO CHANGE

I'm great at resolutions, at amazing (or ridiculous, depending on who you're asking) feats of discipline. Maybe it's because I grew up going to schools that were so strict it was silly: We had a rule against wearing a shirt with one single stripe across it (multiple stripes were fine), a rule against making eye contact with other students in class, and our skirts were measured for length against particular bones in our knees (please don't try to make sense of this). Maybe my addiction to structure is because of my strict school, or maybe it's because I'm German and Protestant and Midwestern. Maybe I'm just weird — likely it's all of the above. Whatever the reason, if we got grades for sticking to New Year's Resolutions, I'd be making straight A's. (It's embarrassing to admit how much I *WISH* we got grades for resolutions.)

In 2011 I made my most successful resolution of all when I started a blog called Shop Small. The concept was pretty simple: I committed to buying everything from locally owned shops for one year and to blogging about my adventures. I made up some rules, like defining "locally-owned" as "Alabama-owned." And I created a couple of loopholes to be sure my friends didn't disown me during the year: I wouldn't turn away gifts bought out of state (as long as I wasn't spending my own money, it was fine), and I had three "wishes" to use each month at a big box store (I ended up using these extremely rarely).

So my commitment wasn't impossible, but you wouldn't have thought that from the amount of pushback I got about it, from the number of people who told me it couldn't be done, or warned that I'd run out of money, or called me stupid and crazy. I also had a few people ask me where I got the idea, like I stole it from some Brooklyn hipster or something. But it was just me: a girl living in Alabama.

I wanted to do something meaningful (my job at the time felt relatively soulless). I wanted to take on a writing project that would make me produce something every day. And I was looking for a new a challenge, too. But my shop small story doesn't really start in 2011. It starts a few years earlier in a little Alabama bookshop.

MY JOURNEY FROM QUIRKY BOOKSELLER TO SLIGHTLY-LESS-QUIRKY BARISTA

I guess it really started when I quit my job at the newspaper. The paper's editor was making decisions I thought were unethical, and since ethics and ideals are pretty much all you have as a journalist (it's not like they pay you well or your industry has a future or anything), I quit. I didn't have a plan, but I did have friends who worked in a little independent bookstore-slash-coffee shop in a small affluent community near Birmingham.

Jonathan Benton, Bookseller had a sort of ramshackle charm and a generous helping of quirky customers, but most importantly, it had health insurance for part-time employees. One short interview and a few kind words about the Queen of England later (the manager was a major Anglophile), I was stamping our logo onto book bags, teaching coworkers how to use Google, drinking my weight in mochas, and borrowing (and reading) a whole lot of books.

It was supposed to be temporary, but I loved it too much. I loved the quiet of the shop before we opened. I loved working side-by-side with fantastic people who became my friends. Looking back, I think working at that shop felt a lot like "playing" shopkeeper: the way little kids pretend with cash registers and Monopoly money. Even when I was promoted to store manager, it didn't seem like a serious business. That was partly because we had no money (not even the Monopoly kind). Actually, we had negative money, so I kept the store afloat by begging my musician friends to play not-strictly-legal shows and charging a cover. When I took over, we had no money even to order books. I always got the employees paid, but there wasn't cash for anything else: My assistant manager and I actually re-numbered old calendars each month because we couldn't afford new ones.

After a year of that, we'd paid all our bills and were in good standing with publishers again, so we could order books. We even sprung for a new calendar! One problem: I was personally $15,000 in credit card debt. I'd paid for so many store supplies with my own money (well, with the credit card company's money), and I wasn't really making a living wage in the first place, so any time I needed groceries, I pulled out the plastic. My debt, combined with the fact that the bookstore's management had changed and I wasn't on board with their plans for the shop, made me motivated to make a change. One particularly rough day at the shop, I took a 20-minute break, hopped on my Vespa, and drove five minutes to the Starbucks that my friend Cal managed. "How do I get a job at Starbucks?" I asked. His answer: "You just did."

I thought working at Starbucks would be a lot different than working for an independent, and in some ways it was. We had more customers, more guidelines and checklists, and more rigidly enforced cleaning procedures. But in a lot of ways that mattered, it wasn't that different from working at an indie bookstore: My Starbucks prioritized customer interaction. We knew the customers, and the customers knew and liked us. We also had a very tight-knit group of employees, and I loved hanging out with them both in and out of the shop, just like I did my coworkers from Jonathan Benton. And my friendships with people from both shops stood the test of time more than almost any other relationships in my life — I still count several of my coworkers as close friends. I knew Starbucks was a corporation, but it never seemed heartless, and the company invested a lot in me: both in the insurance they provided me even as a part-time employee and in the trainings they gave me for free that would later help me build my own business. Of course, Starbucks is a rare corporation. It has its faults, for sure, but for the most part they treat their people and their farmers really well (or at least they did when I worked there). All in all, I'd say my belief that local was always better than big box was a little shaken.

SAVE MONEY, GET HEALTHY, WRITE A BOOK

While I was at Starbucks, I started a blog/contest with my friend and fellow barista Elisa. The concept was simple: We'd compete to see who could spend the least money in three months. And we'd blog about it. We called it Cheap Women (yeah, we did), and we basically tried to practice the highest forms of cheapskatery possible. This led to hijinks such as smuggling vodka into bars in our purses, eating diets primarily comprised of pillaged Starbucks pastries, hand-sewing Christmas gifts out of stolen canvas bank bags, and filling up beer bottles with water so it looked like we were still drinking even when our money had run out. (That last one is a great best practice for staying hydrated while you're out drinking, by the way.) The contest was silly, for sure, but it seriously helped us get our finances in order — Cheap Women is when I actually admitted to and started paying off that huge $15K debt.

Full disclosure: I was secretly hoping that daily blogging at Cheap Women would make me famous. Perhaps unsurprisingly, it did not. What it did was give me a real love for blogging. As a writer, it was great for me to have a daily deadline for getting something on paper (well, on the Internet). And seeing other people enjoy my thoughts, my outlook on life and my sense of humor was incredibly encouraging. Sure, we live in a post-bubble-burst, post-crash world, and as a writer it's particularly difficult to get paid. But it's incredibly easy to publish your work and to put your ideas and your stories into the world. People may not pay for them, but they do read them. To me, that's empowering. It's pretty magical, actually.

Later, I wrote the blog-novel Some New Trend with my friend Kevin. Each week, one of us would write a new chapter of our book, and then we'd blog it. We also podcasted weekly segments of the story as an audiobook, threw a big launch party, wrote dozens of complementary book and music reviews and hosted weekly giveaways. In hindsight, I don't know why we felt like this was a reasonable about of work (we both had full-time jobs), but somehow we pulled it off. Some New Trend taught me that 1) Writing fiction about teens in a mall yields a goldmine of material, 2) Podcasting is a lot of fun, and 3) Boys think nasty jokes are hilarious. (Many times my edits to Kevin's chapters consisted of my repeatedly scribbling "stop it," and "gross-gross-gross-gross" into the margins.)

I also learned that I love blogging with friends ("working collaboratively" is what they'd probably call it in the corporate world). Elisa and I went on to start another blog/contest: this time to break our way into sports that seemed too daunting to try on our own. During Triathablog, I blogged about running, Amanda was our swimmer, and Elisa began her journey into cycling. During the course of this blog, I ran around Birmingham wearing ladybug wings, drank a gallon of water every day for a week, wrote a book report on ultra-marathoners, and ran dressed like an elf on Christmas morning. I also discovered a lot about myself and my relationship with exercise through writing about it, and I got comfortable with running. I certainly didn't become a serious runner, but I'm no longer intimidated by people who are.

But the best thing that came out of our project was that Elisa fell so in love with bicycles that she couldn't stop cycling or writing about them, and she started the blog Bike Skirt with our friend Anna. Bike Skirt is to Triathablog as The Simpsons is to The Tracy Ullman Show — the spinoff is way more popular than its source material. Anna and Elisa (and Alan, another friend of ours) went on to co-found Bici, a Birmingham bicycle co-op. I love that the co-op teaches kids how to fix their own bikes, that they encourage women to pick up wrenches and change tires instead of sitting on the sidelines, and that they work so hard to build a community. I love that they throw fun races and that even I, the amateurest of ama-

teur cyclists, am welcome to hop on my bike and follow
along. What they created is beautiful, and even though
my part in it is only very tiny, I'm proud to be connected
with it at all. Triathablog and Bike Skirt taught me that a
blog can effect real change.

My blogs had goals, but they were mostly personal: Save money, write a book, get healthy. One day, I
stumbled on a blog called Eating Alabama. It's about
four friends who dedicated one whole year to eating only
foods grown in Alabama. Their project was ambitious,
showing how broken our food system has become and
revealing the sad truth that eating locally and staying
healthy is nearly impossible: American food is so out
of whack that if you try to eat locally, even in a fairly
agrarian state like Alabama, there's a good chance you
can't eat many essential foods, and you can forget abou
citrus, tea, or coffee. That causes a problem with gettin
the nutrients you need (Like coffee!), since a lot of the
food we need biologically is trucked across the country
instead of grown locally.

I loved the Eating Alabama project. I found it impo
ant and admirable — but it also left me feeling defeat
I was no stranger to eating mindfully. I'd been a veget
ian for over a decade, a member of a CSA before mos
people had ever heard of one, and I cooked at home
most of the time and grew herbs on my porch. I was

ly educated about my food choices, but Eating Alabama showed me a problem that was much bigger. They did an important work by shining a light on a very broken system. But I felt powerless to change it.

PHILOSOPHER CYCLISTS AND RELUCTANT PROPHETS

Eating Alabama was a great blog, but sometimes reading it felt like a guilt trip, and while guilt can make us feel bad in the moment, I don't think it's a good way to change long-term behavior. For proof, let's look at my bicycle, sitting under its layer of dust. I rarely get on that bike, and it's partly because my friend Neal is so passionate about his. Neal's a hardcore bike commuter who hates cars, even hybrids. Most of the time, he won't even accept a ride in a car, even when we work the same shift and I know he's exhausted or doesn't want to ride home in the rain.

Neal's passion certainly makes me feel bad about myself. As I passively scoot to work on a Vespa, he gets stronger and stronger as he falls off his bike and gets back on, pushes his way up the ridiculous hills that are all over Birmingham, puts up with getting sweaty and getting rained on (sometimes in the same ride), and gets yelled at and run off the road by cars. I'll admit: Neal does a great job of reminding me of the problems with our car-centric culture and our dependence on oil, just like Eating Alabama showed me how broken our food system is. But Neal doesn't make me feel inspired to get on a bike. I just feel overwhelmed.

I'm a passionate and principled person, too, and it's tempting to approach life in this all-or-nothing way. The problem is, I don't think this approach gets results. Passion can easily come across as judgment, and when we insist on a black-and-white outlook, we mostly annoy people instead of changing their minds. Instead of inviting other people to follow, we push them away. And even the people who follow us are likely to get burned out quickly and give up.

I still think there's a place for activism and even extremism. The fact that Neal serves as a constant reminder of what's wrong with oil dependence is a powerful thing and an important thing. The Eating Alabama blog (and their documentary of the same name) points out critical issues in our food system. A strong, unequivocal stance can be just what we need to get people to pay attention, but that doesn't necessarily inspire a change in behavior.

On the other hand, my friend Anna does inspire me

to get on my bike. Out of all my cyclist friends (and, for a non-cyclist, I have a strangely high number of cyclist friends), she's the one who's gotten me on my bike the most, because she doesn't shame me when I don't ride it. She has a car, but most days she bikes. She's extremely active in our local cycling community (she was one-half of Bike Skirt and one of the founding members of the Bici bike co-op), but I've never once heard her give a speech about oil or cuss out a Prius. She encourages me to take easy rides, to bike to breweries (beer at every stop is a powerful motivator), and to have fun. She offers an alternative to all-or-nothing: a little something. The irony is, because she's effecting change both in herself and in me (and others), she ultimately has a bigger impact on saving fuel than Neal does, even though he never uses gas.

When I wondered if there was a way for people (including me) to reform our communities without overhauling our own lives so much, I rediscovered shopping small. Buying locally does require small changes, but it doesn't necessarily involve a lot of suffering. I already knew that a lot more money stays in our communities when we buy local, even if the products aren't local: Eating Alabama might be best, but even if we buy our coffee and carrots and cardamom (Cardamom? I know, I know, but I needed another c-food.) from mom-and-pops, we fund our local economies.

That got me thinking about an idea I'd had years before — to spend a year shopping only at locally owned stores and to blog about what happened. I wanted to let people know they could put more money in their communities by shopping locally, but I also wanted to be honest about the difficult parts: the times when I really missed Target and Netflix and discounts. I thought I could do it, but most of my friends did not. A conversation I had with a friend in a McDonald's (this was during Cheap Women, which I'm hoping explains the McDonald's) was pretty typical: He said the blog, which I'd already named Shop Small, was just too idealistic, too long of a commitment, probably impossible to complete, and above all, too expensive.

I did it anyway.

FASHION SCARES ME MORE THAN ZOMBIES

It took me awhile to find out which stores were local, to switch my shopping, and to establish new habits. It took less time than I'd thought (about two months, when I'd expected it to take a whole year), but the transition wasn't seamless. Mostly, the inconvenience felt less like a hassle and more like an adventure. It made me try new places that gave me new experiences and ended up being pretty rewarding, even for an introvert-hermit like me. (Introvermit? Hervert? Those both sound disgusting, and I should probably stop trying to make this word happen.) As it turns out, breaking out of our habits is good for our brains and our mental states as well as for our local economies. It's healthy to change it up sometimes and get out of our ruts. Shopping small was a great way for me to do that. Of course, not everything went smoothly, and there were a few small shops that I just never warmed up to no matter how hard I tried.

My number one problem: Buying clothes. This isn't because it's difficult to find places to buy clothes locally, but because I'm really, really bad at clothes shopping. Without my twin fashion crutches, Target and the Anthropologie sales closet, I was pretty much lost. Thrift stores, surprisingly, were out, because all I could find were Goodwills and Salvation Armys, and they're not local. (I do understand that any common-sense adaptation of a buy-local lifestyle should probably give charities an exemption. But common sense is not my strong suit.) I did try to shop in boutiques, but I failed pretty miserably.

Most major clothing stores don't carry clothes that fit the average American woman (or that's their biggest size), but boutique clothing tends to be even worse. They carry sizes that are considered "aspirational," which means that they make you want to pull your hoodie around yourself like a blanket and hurry home to hide at the bottom of a carton of Ben and Jerry's. I'm not a large woman, but I'm around the middle of the sizes in a chain store, which puts me completely out of range in a boutique. (Never has the term "small shop" felt more appropriate.) I couldn't bring myself to walk into a room of stick figure sales people and try on their clothing (inevitably, these places have dressing "rooms" that are just hallways with little curtains, so you're already feeling exposed even before you try on the shirt that won't button all the way). I just couldn't handle the judgment, so I didn't even really try. (If you're thinking a real friend wouldn't judge me by the way I look, I'd say that you're correct, and also that you're probably a dude.)

During my formative years, at the age most girls were (I assume) getting schooled on matching patterns and learning to navigate the mall, my mom was pulling hand-me-downs out of the attic. I can rock a pile of my aunt's discarded jumpers like a champ, but put me in the middle of a mall and I totally shut down. You know how men are dragged into stores for what they say feels like hours, and they sit around on those little couches by the dressing rooms looking bored and checking sports scores (or whatever) on their phones? I envy those men. Getting stuck in these stores as a girl with girlfriends who love shopping is much worse, because you can't kick back on the couch (at least, not if you're planning on keeping your friends). I wander around mall stores twice, three times, and even a dozen times, faking interest in this season's denim and becoming increasingly baffled by how my friends could be so intrigued by this clothing. I'd rather read sports scores for two hours than shop for 20 minutes, and I'm not even into sports.

By the time I reached proper adulthood, I'd developed a couple of solutions to my shopping phobia. You can always rely on Target to have some variation of whatever piece of clothing you're looking for, from swimsuit to business suit with everything in between. And for anything more adventurous, I just went to the sales room at Anthropologie or J. Crew. (I guess we're supposed to see sales rooms as discard bins, but I see them as the real store and the rest of the sales floor as expensive museum pieces. Maybe a closet full of cast-offs is closer to the hand-me-down trash bags of my childhood.)

Combined with my personal issues are the insecurities that almost all American women have: I'm obsessed with my weight and convinced that being fat is the worst thing ever. I live under the assumption that I am in fact fat, and that shopping is mostly an exercise in camouflage, hoodwinking the public into believing I'm thinner than I really am. Besides that, pop culture has taught me that I'm supposed to dress just slutty enough that I could be mistaken for a hooker in the right situation, but not so slutty that any girl could reasonably call me a hooker when she's angry. It's quite a fine line, and to a girl like me who's happiest in jeans, converse, a t-shirt and a hoodie, this is a difficult combination to master. Fashion-wise, I should've been born an overweight male who likes to write computer code and play World of Warcraft. (I don't mean that as an insult to programmers or gamers. Seriously, man — I like your shirt.)

I did buy clothes during my Shop Small year. I bought them at Zoes, a consignment shop near my house. They didn't always have what I was looking for, and their shop cat always made me sneeze. The only things they consistently had in stock were fishnets and tutus (except, ironically, when I needed a tutu for Mardi Gras, and then I couldn't find one). But the staff was always nice and helpful, the sales were plentiful (and applied to the entire store, not just one little room), and I found that, as long as I stopped in regularly, I'd hit Zoes on a day when someone my size and style had just left, and then I'd find some fantastic pieces. They did have those stupid curtain rooms, but I can be flexible. I ended up getting more clothes than I'd ever gotten in past years, and most of them were from higher-end labels than what I'd bought before. And I got it all for less money, too.

MY KINGDOM FOR A STAPLER!

Of course, the year wasn't all roses and shop cats. Sometimes small stores let me down, and sometimes I bailed on them. The only thing I really, truly could never find at a local store during Shop Small were office supplies. No toner, no photo paper, no paperclips, no staplers. I'd find odds and ends at high-end stationary shops or locally owned drugstores, but in general I was out of luck. No printer ink anywhere. For a writer, that's a pretty big problem.

For the most part, I stole printer paper and copies from my desk job. It was a solution, I guess, but not a good one. Beyond outright thievery, I also tried just making due — printing on both sides of the paper, using old notepads, getting every last bit of ink out of the pens. I don't see a local shop carrying office supplies any time soon, since companies like Office Max presumably get much bigger wholesale discounts. I'm glad I was forced to re-use more (Hurray, Earth!), but it got to be pretty annoying.

Electronics, including computers, are usually hard to find from small shops, too. I bought computer hardware, including the iPad that I used to read locally purchased Kobo ebooks, from locally owned Perry Computer. I always get fantastic service there (even without an appointment — take that, Apple Store), one of their employees reminds me of Olivander from Harry Potter (definitely a plus for me), and they even let me know when another shop has a better deal than they do. I think that kind of service is way better than price-matching. I got pretty lucky with my computer and even with other electronics that I needed (which I found at a local hardware store). Typically, though, these are two areas that make shopping small challenging.

Independent shopping failed me on the office supplies front, but I failed it when it came to movies. I felt like I was in the good graces of the universe when an independent theater opened in my town right around the same time I started my blog. The problem? I hardly ever went. One reason was completely my fault: I could never find it. I'm directionally challenged, and the theater is tucked away in a weird spot (you try using Google Maps while driving a Vespa). But the real reason is that I never had a good experience when I went. I'm really picky when it comes to movies. I want the theater to be comfortable, clean and cold. I should need to put a sweater on and feel wrapped in a cocoon of warmth and story. (Yes, I realize this is a waste of energy, and wanting it anyway undoes all the environmental good I did reusing printer paper.) When I've paid $15 to sit in a perfectly controlled movie theater and that experience is ruined, I'm not a happy person.

Maybe it's my bad luck, but it seems like something always goes wrong at the independent theater. I sat through movies there where a baby was loudly crying for half the movie and the managers (and the mother) did nothing. (One of those movies was the new Harry Potter, and I now think ruining a midnight release of a Harry Potter movie by bringing your baby deserves punishment by an unforgivable curse.) I had a friend who saw a movie there when the lights didn't go down at all. I've even had friends caught in a weird mob/riot situation at this theater. All in all, I just didn't have a good experience, and I ended up spending more of my "wishes" on seeing movies at bigger theaters just to avoid the independent.

Netflix was another crutch for me. Since Blockbuster and pretty much every other video rental place got shut down by those little red envelopes, there's not local place to rent movies anymore, and I thought I'd be limited to the library's DVD collection for twelve months. This both panicked and interested me. Everyone's a Netflix junkie now, since House of Cards and Orange Is the New Black became the shows to watch, but I joined back in 2001 when most people didn't even have a DVD player. I was living in a cabin in the woods (still within Birmingham city limits — it was a strange situation), and I didn't have a television, or even heat in my apartment other than a wood-burning stove, but I did have Netflix: that's how high a priority it was for me. I mentioned to a few of my friends that I'd be giving up Netflix because of Shop Small, and they pitched in and bought me a year's subscription for Christmas. It was a thoughtful gift, and I didn't want to be rude, so I used it. I'm sure it made my year a lot more pleasant, and technically it didn't break my rules, since I didn't pay for it, but I've always been disappointed in myself for not lining my big-screen choices up with my shop small goals.

HOPING FOR THE WORST (IT MAKES A BETTER STORY)

I figured creating an interesting plot for my blog-story would be easy. I'd thought most of my purchases would be hard to find, requiring a lot of unsuccessful searching and going without. I also thought I could whine about how much I missed big box stores: Filling a red basket at Target makes me really happy. I've always felt comfortable and at home at Barnes and Noble. And walking into Whole Foods is like crossing into a magical world where lumberjack-style men stack avocados into perfect pyramids, where hot punk-rock guys help me pick out aged cheese, where cute boys with beards make me delicious juice drinks (if you're guessing I have an obsession with the men of Whole Foods, you are not wrong), and where health and happiness seem as close as the maple syrup aisle. I anticipated all kinds of problems with small shopping, from running out of money to going into grocer-crush withdrawal, and I thought all these issues would translate into plot twists that would make writing Shop Small easy and fun.

It didn't exactly turn out that way. Despite a handful of exceptions, like staplers, shopping locally wasn't nearly as annoying as I'd expected, and most of the time I found a replacement for corporate shopping quickly and easily. For example, I'd thought I'd be getting gas at Munchies, a gas station a few minutes away from my house. The main thing about Munchies that's good is that they sell cigarettes late into the night, and they're next to Parkside, one of my favorite bars. Munchies is obviously locally owned, because no company with any connection to oil money would let Munchies fall into its current state of complete disrepair. As I picture

Munchies right now, I see the sign hanging off its hinges, quietly squeaking into the night. (I'm exaggerating, but it's that kind of place.) I steeled myself to start filling up at Munchies, but I wasn't happy about it. First of all, I'm a little frightened of Munchies. Second, it seemed silly and wasteful to drive a couple of miles out of my way, right past a Chevron, to get gas.

Before I started trekking out to Munchville, I called my friend John, who owned a gas station at the time. I won't get into how weird that was, since John was my age, and I didn't think people my age should be owning gas stations. He was also a graphic designer, a screen printer, and a bonafide hipster with a fauxhawk and a penchant for Christian hardcore music and Mac computers. John doesn't seem like your typical gas station owner, but that's one thing you learn early when you shop small — small business owners generally don't match their stereotypes. They're kind of an odd, quirky bunch.

Anyway, John did own a gas station, so I gave him a call. He explained, to my surprise, that most gas stations are locally owned. They have those big signs reading BP, Shell and Chevron because they sign really long contracts with the gas companies, and the signs are part of the deal. Sometimes those deals are good, and sometimes they're bad — just ask any locally owned gas station that had a BP sign after the oil spill. Buying gas from a local shop was actually really easy. I just walked in and asked whoever was working if the store was locally owned. I'm happy to report that almost every gas station I walked into was local.

As it turns out, I was wrong about a lot of things, and not all of them had to do with fuel. Finding all my favorite items did take a little searching, but after a couple of months I had it sorted out and had arranged my life into new patterns that made shopping just as easy as it ever was. I didn't miss shopping at big box stores nearly as much as I'd thought I would, and I actually enjoyed the adventure of shopping at new ones. I loved stumbling on original and fun local shops that I would've passed by before. It felt like going on a treasure hunt, and more often than not, I struck gold — and for much less money than I'd imagined.

CARRIE ROLLWAGEN

LOCAL SHOPPING HACKS: A BRIEF GUIDE TO SHOPPING SMALL

Shopping small is easier than I thought; it really boils down to doing a little bit of research to find out which stores are local, and being willing to try new things, to find new places and to make new discoveries. But I found a few strategies to make that process even easier:

SHOP LOCAL-ISH.

Getting so frustrated that you quit isn't going to help. Going cold turkey on big box shops can be tough, especially if you live in a town that doesn't have many locally owned stores. Switch a few of your purchases immediately, and keep making small changes. They have a way of adding up. We tend to think of big box stores first, and only shop small when we don't have any other choice. We can make powerful change just by flip-flopping: shopping small first, and buying corporate only as a last resort.

ASK LOCAL.

Independent shop owners and workers are generally pretty knowledgeable about other local shops in their town, partly because local buying is an obvious priority in their lives, and because they probably network with other business owners through neighborhood associations, zoning commission meetings and Chamber of Commerce meetings. If you're trying to buy locally and you're having trouble finding what you're looking for, ask the owner of a small shop you trust. They'll probably help you out, especially if you're making a purchase. (Also, mentioning that buying local is important to you often wins points from a small shop owner.)

HELP YOURSELF.

As proof that the measure of a tool is in how we use it, the same Internet that gave us cyber shopping and Amazon's Super Saver Shipping can also be an asset for small shopping. Google the name of the product you're looking for with the name of your city, and you'll often find local shops offering what you want. Follow your favorite locally owned shops and restaurants on social media to find out what they have to offer and when they're having sales and specials (you can also use social media to ask questions of local shops directly, or to ask your friends and followers about their favorite local spots). The Internet is usually a good resource for learning more about a shop and finding out if it's locally owned, since most stores have websites that either list that information (if they link out to a parent corporation or lots of additional locations, that's usually a bad sign) or provide contact numbers so you can find it for yourself.

HELP SMALL SHOPS.

Use your social media to post pictures when you shop locally and eat at local restaurants. "Bragging" about where you've been is a great way to encourage others to shop small without being preachy. There's no need to post a picture every time you visit a small shop, but do it when you find something you really love, when you discover a great new boutique or have the greatest sandwich of your life at a local restaurant. These little snapshots from your life help your friends get to know new shops, and they encourage others to shop small and post about their adventures as well. Plus, posting pictures from your visit to a local restaurant is great karma and makes the shop owner feel fantastic.

THE LOCALIST

DOLLAR MENU MILLIONAIRES: HOW FAST FOOD AND DISCOUNTS KEPT ME POOR

My fear of not having enough money was the main reason I didn't start Shop Small earlier. Pretty much everyone I asked about the project had the same viewpoint: It would be crazy, and it would be expensive. I personally thought spending so much money would be interesting from a narrative perspective. I already knew from Cheap Women that writing about the semi-impoverished lifestyle (well, as semi-impoverished as middle-class white Americans get, which admittedly is a misuse of the word "impoverished") would be compelling to a blog readership. The tougher it was to make ends meet, the better my blog would be. That's why I waited to start the blog until I'd already paid off my credit card debt and landed a steady, well-paying job; I finally thought I could afford it. And if I was wrong? Well, as a vegetarian, I was already used to eating a lot of beans.

In fact, I spent less money in my year of shopping small than I had in any other year since I graduated college. And it was a good thing, too, because my job situation changed, and I ended up making only $13,000 for an entire year. I did have a little bit of savings, and

73

my parents kicked in as much as they could, but that added up to a couple thousand altogether. I think almost anyone would agree that living on that little money is a substantial feat, and it means something real had changed in my spending patterns. It wasn't a fluke, but it went against common sense. How did this happen? I have a few ideas.

There's an old trick that's supposed to stop you from spending money: You freeze your credit card in a big block of ice (I think I saw this on Oprah). The idea is that you have to wait for the ice to melt to use your card, and by the time that happens you will have talked yourself out of making any impulse purchases. Shopping small was my big block of ice. Whenever I needed something, I had to figure out where I could purchase it, since there's no locally owned equivalent to Target. Instead of heading immediately across town, I'd usually wait until I'd be in that area anyway. Say, for example, I needed chalkboard paint and I wanted to get my shoes repaired. I'd do them in the same trip, since a nearby neighborhood has both a locally owned hardware store and a couple of local cobblers. Combining trips to nearby places just made sense. But here's the thing — over half the time, waiting would make me realize that I didn't really "need" an item in the first place. I mean, no one actually *NEEDS* chalkboard paint (sorry to break it to you, Pinterest junkies).

Once I gave myself a day to think about the purchase, I talked myself out of it. I started to understand that many of my purchases were emotional, and I learned (for the most part) to deal with my frustrations in other ways. Essentially, I was less likely to impulse buy or to buy anything frivolous because I was more likely to plan.

Impulse buys, as it turns out, were my financial Kryptonite. When people ask me how my debt got to its pre-Cheap Women $15K level, I tell them I bought a lot of ranch fries. This is kind of a joke, but what I mean is that I made small, seemingly insignificant purchases that really added up. I bought ranch fries from The Purple Onion. I bought Hello Kitty notebooks at Target. I bought gum at the grocery store. I bought Hello Kitty-printed socks. (I had a little problem for awhile there; that cat is just very cute.) Basically, I made a lot of impulse purchases that really added up. The bulk of my purchases were not planned for — I took them home when fate brought us together in the checkout aisle … and by fate, I mean a highly paid psychological marketer whose job is to predict and exploit customer purchasing patterns.

Corporations make careful plans to encourage us to purchase: from their displays to their shelving to the layout of their stores. But where big box stores have cash register kiosks packed with grab-and-go products, your local shop is more likely to have a Take-a-Penny tray and a pile of fliers for a free art show next to their register. Most small business owners don't hire psychological marketers (because they can't afford it, not because they're above it or anything). A shopkeeper is more likely to be a jack-of-all-trades than a master of the art of manipulation.

Your average small shop isn't going to try to sell you a store credit card (or even a loyalty card). You can't pick a soda out of the refrigerator when you leave, and they're not going to try to upsell you on a boxed set of Dexter. I found that, even when I wanted to buy a little something extra because I had a rough day or thought I deserved a treat, that was hard to accomplish. I almost always left only with what I needed. My impulses were drowned out by the logic that reminded me my budget couldn't take the hit of extra purchasing, and both my bank account and my amount of free time grew because I learned to prioritize my purchases.

Superstores spend thousands of dollars figuring out not only which products they'll carry, but also where those products should be stocked for maximum sales. This type of coercion is effective partly because it's designed not to be noticed. You probably think you're not like me, and that you're not swayed by advertising and that you don't spend much on impulse buys, but it's a lot more likely you do exactly the same thing. (Except probably with fewer appearances from Hello Kitty.) I'm not the only person who buys on impulse, racks up credit debt, and uses money to curb emotional problems. If I were, our local, national and global economies wouldn't be in the trouble they're in now. Our whole world has been looking at money backward and betting on a future windfall that will probably never come instead of living within our means.

It makes sense to think shopping locally is expensive. Per-product, it usually is. Most items are either more expensive or the same price at local shops, and not as many small shops have discount clubs and bonus buys and incentive programs. But small shops are also less likely to encourage impulse buying, or to incentivize us to buy more than we can afford using credit or to trick us with hidden fees. Those big box policies allow them to advertise rock-bottom prices while they're really shoving us off a financial cliff.

Sometimes I did have to go without during my year of shopping small, but that wasn't the chore or the punishment that I'd thought it would be. It was actually kind of nice to deal with a lack of money by not buying anything instead of by racking up credit card debt that ultimately made my problems worse.

THE GOOD, THE BAD AND THE CORPORATE

Cutting down on impulse buying, upping the planning and cutting down on emotional purchases certainly helped me save money. But the real change, the lasting change, is that I began to understand that my money has meaning, and it actually connects me to people and my community. As a society, we're taught to be disconnected from money: We swipe plastic instead of spending cash. We borrow instead of saving. We're told that personal changes are small and meaningless on a global scale. Shopping small reveals how misleading that disconnect is.

The changes in the global economy that come from local shopping may take awhile, but the changes in the personal economies of the people who own and run small shops are obvious immediately. We see smiles on the faces of cashiers because our purchases give them money to feed their families. We're greeted by name on the third trip back to the same grocery store. When we visit that local restaurant more than once, they remember our orders. And proprietors and employees of local establishments start to smile and say hello when we see them around town. Suddenly, we're connected, and we realize

that we have been all along, but we didn't feel it before.
When we see that our money has a real, immediate impact, and that it can make people's lives better instead
of just pushing the decimal another place to the right
on a corporate spreadsheet, we understand our money
better. And that means we spend it better too.

The best way to be sure money stays in our communities, of course, is to buy local AND to buy American, to
be sure both the products we buy and the stores we buy
them from are benefitting our country and our communities. Buying American stimulates innovation by keeping
both the labor and creative class at home; it necessitates
a better-paid labor force; and it creates jobs for all of us.
But it isn't practical or advisable to ignore the fact that
we live in a global economy, and we've reached a point
where it's almost impossible for Americans to buy only
products made in the U.S. (especially since most of us,
including me, are hooked on foreign-made electronics).
I'm not about impossible goals. I'm about small changes
that have big results.

Simply making the change to buy from local shops
has a tremendous impact on strengthening our economy
and creating jobs. Most Americans are busy and stressed
and worried, and it's not practical for most of us to go
a year without big box shopping. I don't want to shame
people for not buying locally; it's mean, and I don't think

it's effective. What is effective is making small changes and building on them — buying localish until we become localists. Going cold-turkey from corporate stores isn't the best idea for everyone. We can't (and shouldn't) all be anarchists — it can be just as brave to fight for balance and reasonable change, and we just might get better results.

When I started the Shop Small blog, I wanted to be even more balanced. I'd planned on having good things and bad things to say about both big box stores and small shops. But when I looked at the facts, small shops were the clear winners: both for the community and for me as a consumer. For one thing, the small shops had a lot more to offer, both from their stock and from their staff, than I'd given them credit for. And I also learned some pretty nasty things about the big corporations I'd grown to love, even those I'd considered good: During the Shop Small year, some of the best and most professional people I've ever worked with were fired by Starbucks, a corporation I'd embraced. One of my best friends was repeatedly harassed by her employers at Urban Outfitters (part of the same company as my beloved Anthropol-ogie). As I explored the subject, I learned that these problems weren't just unfortunate quirks of the corporate system — they were at the root of the system.

But the more I talked, the less people listened to me.

The prophet may help you see the truth, but that light hurts, especially when we've all been in the dark for too long. When I wrote Shop Small, I often felt alone — but I know that feeling was more insecurity than truth. In reality, other people were fighting with me, and they were working to make things better, too. I have to believe that our voices, even though they're small, will make a difference. I have to believe that people, even just a few of us, are more powerful than a corporation.

BRINGING BACK THE MAGIC

A few years ago, I visited the village of Hogsmeade from the Harry Potter books. It was just a theme park in Orlando, but as soon as I walked through the gates, the magic felt real, and it felt infectious. All along the stone streets, people looked happy. We talked to each other. We broke into smiles. As we peered into shop windows filled with magic wands, cauldrons and potion ingredients, we stopped to help each other take snapshots, complimenting strangers on their Hufflepuff shirts and Gryffindor scarves, and talking with the vendors standing behind carts loaded with Pumpkin Juice and Butterbeer.

What really struck me about the Wizarding World

(besides the Butterbeer, which was super delicious) was that it isn't all that magical. Mostly, it's a simple street filled with charming independent shops. Hand-painted shingles hang from the awnings. Shopkeepers sweep up their doorsteps and shout cheerful greetings. Sure, some of the shops had magical displays, like the musical instruments that play themselves, but mostly they were just quirky and unique and bursting with personality. I was charmed (and I was geeking out — I love Harry Potter), but I was also a little bit sad to realize that we've come so far from the fabled Main Streets of our past that visiting small shops seems as foreign as time-traveling witches and shape-shifting cats.

At home, we don't shop like this. When we go to the store or the mall, we have tunnel vision. We power walk. There's no talking to strangers, and there's certainly no chatting with the people handing us our Cokes and fries. We've forgotten what it means to saunter, to connect, to enjoy.

But that doesn't mean we can't get those things back. If we take pride in craftsmanship again, we might be a little more content with what we have instead of scrambling for more. If our towns and neighborhoods felt more unique and personal, we might work harder to make them even better and stronger. Maybe small shops really do have their own magic, and maybe that's something we can get back. The more I looked into buying locally, the more I saw that it's not just about having charming shops full of personality. It is about that, but it's also about putting more support and more money back into our communities where it belongs. It's also about dismantling a corporate system that's made doing good difficult, that's separated us from our neighbors, that's taken away our personhood and our choices and made us lonely in the process.

I know as well as anyone that this can be overwhelming, but it doesn't have to be. In order to be localists, we just have to start shopping local-ish. If we think independent first, and buy corporately only as a last resort; if we start to prioritize buying our art and our food locally; if we make a few small changes to our lives and keep adding to those, I really believe our cities and towns will get stronger. We have the money that makes corporate America run, and we can take it away. We have voices that matter, and we can save our small shops and build our communities in the process. Harry Potter taught me that no spell can bring back the dead. Lucky for us, America's independents aren't dead yet.

See that Starbucks over there? Know what it used to be?

— Phil Dunphy

An orange grove?

— Luke Dunphy

No, a Burger King. You can still see some of the architecture.

— Phil Dunphy

Modern Family

CHAPTER THREE

****

THERE GOES THE NEIGHBORHOOD:

How Corporations
Change Community

****

CARRIE ROLLWAGEN

THE INVISIBLE HAND OF THE MARKET GETS ITS PALM GREASED

My grandparents are conservative Republicans in every sense of the word. They buy American, speak out against welfare, invest in oil companies, go to church every Sunday and listen to conservative commentary every day. They also built their own business, their own dream home and a big, happy family. They've lived the American dream, and in a lot of ways, I've followed in their footsteps: I've built my own career, and I care a lot about history and about my country. But I'm also single, I don't have kids, I voted for Obama, and the last time I listened to Rush Limbaugh was when he was being mocked on The Colbert Report. Just as my life looks different than theirs, the way I express my patriotism and citizenship looks different, too.

During the year I was shopping exclusively locally, I was surprised at how many people called me a liberal. It's true that shopping small supports individuals and communities, and that it ultimately increases tax revenue so the government has more money to spend, so in those ways it can support a Democratic agenda. But it was disconcerting to hear so many so-called fiscal conservatives considering buying local to be a liberal cause since effecting change through commerce is essentially a capitalistic endeavor. It seems like the Conservative Right is confused about the very principles they seem to be so passionate about.

True capitalism requires the freedom of the individual to choose which businesses and products to support. As with all freedom, it involves a heavy dose of personal responsibility. It's not about making sure the big businesses have the freedom to grow as big as possible — it's about allowing us, the consumers, to choose which ones get bigger instead of allowing the government to decide for us. But now government regulations and ridiculous tax standards mean big businesses are almost always favored over small ones. That's not a free market. That's not capitalism. That's government manipulation of the market, pure and simple.

Far from standing up for freedom, the GOP preaches zero government and zero compromise while bowing to corporate interests even when they stifle competition and subvert capitalism. We've been so busy making sure government isn't controlling us that we haven't noticed that corporations are controlling us now. Our politicians not only allow big business to do pretty much whatever it wants; now the government actually subsidizes big businesses as they push independents out of business. That's a market that's manipulated in favor of corporations. That's not a free market; that's just socialism for businesses.

In order to do everything a strong country does, things even most Republicans agree with, like going to war and building Interstates and getting murderers off the streets, we need money in our budgets. This is true on a community level as well: Our local governments need money to fix potholes and fund education. No matter your opinion of immigration or abortion or the appropriate level of taxation, if you're in favor of any kind of government at all, it makes sense to be sure our tax money is funneled into our governments (both state and federal) and not overseas. Unfortunately, the money we pour into corporations generally skips the tax system (a lot of it does, anyway), and goes across an ocean. It certainly gives almost nothing back to our small communities.

Our state and community governments are underfunded while our federal government seems bloated and ineffective. The no-compromise, nouveau-libertarian Tea Party has responded by claiming that abundance of government is the biggest problem in our country, that taxes are immoral, and that a true patriot's mission is to chip away at government, piece by piece if necessary, until there's almost nothing left. They choke compromise in the hope that a true, better America will emerge.

These Tea Partiers look to the Boston Tea Party as

their inspiration and their namesake, but they forget that the Bostonians weren't just protesting the Crown of England; they were also opposed to the actions of the East India Company whose monopoly on tea and collusion with the government caused the taxation problem in the first place. Our modern Tea Partiers are out of line not only because they strong-arm polarizing politics through Congress (although that's part of it), but because they're missing half the point of the original rebellion in Boston: That corporate abuse is just as much of a problem as an overbearing government. Far from preventing corporate control, Tea Partiers actually encourage it, lifting restrictions against corporations and favoring big business interests over local entrepreneurs.

I sometimes vote with Republicans, and I sometimes vote Democrat. It's not because I'm moderate, because I'm actually very passionate about the issues I believe in. But most of the time, the Republican ticket no longer reflects the issues that the Grand Old Party is supposed to stand for. My choice is now between a liberal ticket that advocates socialism for people and a Republican ticket that promotes socialism for businesses. Given those options, I'll vote for people. Not because I think socialism works, but because giving welfare to huge corporations — at the expense of our small businesses, our communities and our poor — seems a little bit evil.

It's not good for us as a nation to be so ignorant about what our political parties stand for: Standing up against corporate abuse isn't liberal because it's pro-capitalism. And it is liberal because it helps people. It isn't just a Tea Party concern, but it should be a Tea Party concern, because it's an American concern. Shopping locally means standing up for individual liberty, for the rights of the states, and for fiscal responsibility, and all that is important regardless of political affiliation.

MAGIC BEANS AND TRICKY TAXES

As a kid, I wanted to be President. I'm not sure if that's because I actually like politics (I do), or because I got really into whatever biography I happened to be reading (I did — I also wanted to be a scientist and a nurse and go live on a prairie), or because Ronald Reagan seemed to get all the Jelly Bellies he ever wanted. Probably it was all of the above.

Besides jelly beans, Reagan was really big on Trickle-Down Economics, a concept that's been praised or maligned by pretty much everyone under the political sun. (Is there a political sun? Seems like we'd be in a bad spot if the sun filibustered. Or went into recess.) Whatever your thoughts on Trickle-Down Economics, it doesn't really hold up when corporations hide on the other side of the world and cheat the tax system. The idea that money can flow all the way through the global machine and then come back to us doesn't work out when loopholes and bailouts keep certain parts of the economy artificially inflated. If it ever functioned properly, Trickle-Down Economics certainly won't work when profits are siphoned back into the same big companies that generated them in the first place.

Big corporations are more likely to bend (or break) the tax code because the loopholes they find expand exponentially when they're multiplied by hundreds of divisions and branches in their chains. Small shops don't usually have the resources (money, accounting divisions) to find ways to manipulate the system in the first place, and their incentive to do it is lower, since the money is only saved once. The result is that big box stores rarely pay what they're expected to.

The ways corporations manipulate the tax system are wildly varied and creative, and they end up sounding a little like riddles: Through inversions (also called corporate desertions), a large corporation like Apple sells itself to a small, off-shore company that's located in a country that will let them circumvent tax law or pay less than our IRS will. The company still maintains its U.S. operations and uses our roads and health care and freedom and all that jazz, but they turn into corporate vampires, drawing from the system without paying anything back.

Then there's the pixie dust that is cyberselling. As consumers, buying online makes us feel magical and special. It's a lot like magic for corporations too: They get to avoid the overhead of brick-and-mortar stores (including taxes and utility costs), and they can generally pay warehouse employees less than their in-store counterparts. Beyond that, there's a neat little tax trick corporations have managed to pull off. It goes like this: They don't pay taxes. Okay, it's a little more complicated, but not by much. According to our laws, companies only have to pay taxes on online items purchased by people in the states where the company has a physical base. For example, if Amazon has a warehouse in Kansas, they'll have to pay taxes on items bought by Kansans. (Shout out to Kansans! Rock Chalk Jayhawk!) But on items bought by people in states without a physical base or warehouse (a.k.a., most of them), the corporation isn't responsible for paying taxes — we are. Legally, we as individuals are expected to calculate the taxes on our out-of-state purchases and pay for them each April. As you'd probably guess, this happens about never. In theory, online taxes get paid by individuals once a year. In fact, corporations basically wave a magic wand to make them disappear.

This is why websites can offer such low prices and all the free shipping you can ask for — because they're stealing the money from us in the first place.

Tax revenue from big businesses is also lower because of the money our local governments pay them to get established in the first place. Politicians use deductions, tax exemptions and other financial incentives as bait to try to attract big box stores to their states. They buy the magic beans, rolling over and accepting anything big business wants, just hoping to get face-time with the giant and hopefully share in his profits. What they forget is that giants aren't generally known for their equitable polities and fairness in sharing: All those incentives usually backfire, eating into, or even eliminating, the revenue that made the corporation so attractive in the first place. If local governments took their money and incentives and gave them to local businesses instead, the effect would be bigger and better for local communities in the long run. So why doesn't that happen? Because tracking the effect of several local businesses is more difficult than looking at the statistics from one Wal-Mart. Long-term changes are harder to prove and explain than the appearance of short-term success, and that kind of change doesn't show up in one election cycle. Investing in small shops would have an exponentially greater benefit for the community, but it wouldn't show proven results in time for politicians running for additional terms in office.

It's clear that corporations, for the most part, aren't interested in creating communities. Their responsibility is to shareholders, not to customers, and that's a distinction that comes through in small and big ways every day. Cracking down on corporate tax breaks or encouraging state support of local businesses isn't a project any politician who's seriously interested in reelection (or in continuing to collect money from powerful big-business lobbies) is going to touch. It's up to us as citizens to find creative ways of being involved in our communities, to remember that every dollar we spend in a small shop helps create a better way of life for us and everyone around us. The government is supposed to allocate money where it's best for the country, but in practice the money usually goes to whoever has the loudest lobbyist. If we want to change it, we have to work from the local level. We start at the grassroots. We start with each ten-dollar bill.

BREAKING IT DOWN: HOW MONEY STAYS LOCAL

Why does shopping locally even matter? We could go over graphs and statistics, but that would be boring (to me, at least). Instead, let's say I give you a $10 bill. (Heyyyy, book refund!) When you spend that $10 at Wal-Mart or another big retailer, about $1 to $3 goes back into your community. The rest goes into the big, bad world of international retail. Or maybe it's not a bad world, but the point is, only about $3 of your money, tops, stays in your neighborhood, your city or your state to improve the services that directly effect your life.

Now let's say you have another $10 bill. (You're welcome! I'm incredibly generous in metaphors.) This time you bypass the big box stores and spend your cash in a locally owned grocery or pet shop or coffee shop — whatever. In a locally owned store, anywhere from $4 to $7 re-circulates in your local economy, funding all that quality-of-living stuff like stoplights and hospitals.

Like most of us who came out of an American school system, math isn't my strong suit, but this one's pretty simple: Every time we spend $10 at a locally owned store, anywhere from $1 to $6 *MORE* goes back into our local economies than if we spent the same cash at a corporately owned store. We're not talking decimal points of shifty numbers on a spreadsheet here — this is substantial cash, and it adds up. Say you spend $20,000 a year on things like food, rent and insurance. Making the choice to spend that money locally means, at the very least, 2,000 more dollars a year in your local community. And that number could go as high as $14,000.

Sound too good to be true? That's what I thought, too.

I'm a natural cynic, so the claim that our government gets tons more money just because we buy stuff from local stores seems unbelievable. How could the difference in revenue be so big between buying from a mom-and-pop and a corporate store, especially when we're buying the same products? The answer is less in dollar bills and more in nickels and dimes (or more in decimals than dollars, if you'd like to keep your monetary metaphors digital). Small shops are different in lots of, well, small ways, all the way from whom they hire to how they pay taxes to what kinds of merchandise they stock. Not all local shops are created equal, of course, so the amount of money that actually goes back into the community is going to vary depending on which choices each shop makes — which is why the number fluctuates. The recipe for higher local tax revenue has different ratios depending on the business, but here are the ingredients that are generally involved:

SMALL SHOPS EMPLOY MORE LOCAL PEOPLE.

A big company is likely to ship its brightest minds off to corporate headquarters, but local shops have local staff. Those staff members pay taxes locally, and when they buy groceries and gas and pay rent locally, some of each team member's money gets re-circulated into the community.

BRICK-AND-MORTAR SHOPS PAY LOCAL RENT.

They also pay for power, insurance, Internet and property taxes. (Corporate brick-and-mortars do this, too, but only for their storefronts; their headquarters and warehouses — i.e. the bulk of their businesses — are usually located out-of-state.) Local stores are also more likely to shop for local vendors to do their initial build-outs, make repairs to their buildings, and to buy raw materials for repairs and building projects in-state.

LOCAL SHOPS BUY FROM LOCAL SHOPS.

Businesses sell things to make money, but they also have to spend money on furnishings, office supplies and ingredients, and small businesses are more likely to buy

those things from other small businesses. Do small shops
buy from other small shops because of an ethical code
of buying locally? Sometimes, but usually it's just more
convenient — when it's time to stock inventory, outfit
their offices, or call for repairs, small businesses who buy
from other indies usually get better price negotiation and
more favorable delivery times. And each time the money
passes through another link in the local chain without
circling the globe, more of the original purchase stays at
home.

SMALL SHOPS PAY HIGHER TAXES.
And we already know why.

THE ARCHITECTURE OF CORPORATE AMERICA

It's not just the disappearing revenue streams that
make big box stores problematic. Their personalized, in-
dividualistic version of shopping feels comfortable in the
moment, but it ultimately creates an isolation that isn't
good for us as people. Good urban planning is important
for functional communities and for healthy individuals.
That means we benefit from shopping communities that

are conveniently walkable: The more walking, shopping and interacting we do, the better off we are. Why? We're healthier, because we're walking more. We're happier, because we're communicating with each other (and because we're walking more and experiencing nature more). And our communities are stronger, both in personal ties (because we're communicating) and in tax dollars (because walkable communities and local stores increase community revenues). The corporate model breaks us from this pattern and discourages us from breathing fresh air, exercising and being social.

Big box stores, those behemoths crouched in the middle of parking lots, are part of the problem. Products at Wal-Mart are easy to find because they're boxed up and stacked in a line. This is really convenient when you want to find a light bulb, but it may not be a good template for our cities and towns, or for our humanity. Part of the trouble with the big box model is that it spreads like a weed, consuming not just the inside aisles but the store itself and its surrounding area: Wal-Marts aren't surrounded by trees, ponds and walking paths; they're surrounded by boxy architecture so bland that what used to be our communities can now be confused with a line of cereal boxes on the discount aisle. As most any designer or architect will tell you, this kind of monotony effects our psyches. A world devoid of curves and plants is bad for us as people, and putting efficiency and practicality before beauty has led to an ugly landscape that could have more than just aesthetic consequences, because an abandoned superstore can't be retrofitted into something else.

Those massive parking lots and proprietary designs make big box stores almost impossible to assimilate back into a more natural community design (some abandoned malls and Wal-Marts are converted into churches or libraries, but most are not). Big box stores aren't just too big to fail — they're too ugly to fail, because without the golden halo of discounts, Sam's Club, Lowes and Target look really, really bad. When a superstore is built, we all assume it will never leave, but these stores leave all the time: some to build a bigger store down the road, some because of low profits, and some because they can't bully local authorities the way they'd like. We welcome superstores with open arms, seeing them as a bright shining hope for a better economy, assuming they'll create jobs — and ignoring the fact that those jobs are paying less and less. But superstores are subject to the ebb and flow of the market and to the whims of their leaders just like any other business. They can and do leave. And when they do, it's the community that's punished.

Yes, small shops are sometimes located in strip malls. Yes, independents sometimes personalize their

buildings in not-so-charming ways, making it tough to
find new tenants when they leave, and even small stores
can create blight and waste. But it happens far less.
Most locally owned stores lack the budgets and political
pull to level existing buildings and put up expensive,
logo-dotted boxes. Most independents can't bully zoning
commissions. And it's in the best interest of local shops
to use local contractors (they're cheaper and more convenient), to choose building materials based on accessi-
bility, and to hire local architects and designers who are
familiar with their neighborhoods and better equipped to
take the character of the community into consideration.
Independents aren't perfect, but it's corporations who
are driving the movement for ugly, wasteful, non-livable
stores. They're the ones keeping us in our cars and away
from our neighbors.

I drive a Vespa instead of a car. It's fun and it saves
me gas money, but a lot of days I miss having a car.
There are rainy days and cold days, sure. Winter pretty
much sucks. But beyond that, I miss the air-conditioned, private little cocoon of my car. I miss singing bad
music at the top of my lungs. I miss having a Starbucks
mocha in the cup holder and a Cream Cheese Danish
in its paper wrapping in the center console — all ready
to help me load up on sugar and caffeine before a long
day at work. A car is a respite of sorts for many of us,

and it's no wonder: the world outside can get pretty ugly. Especially if the world outside is a big box store or a strip mall.

Strip malls, and drive-thrus in particular, encourage us to stay in our cocoons. They make us selfish, and they keep us from interacting with each other and with other local shops. We think we like drive-thrus because they're quick, but in fact we'd almost always save time and beat the car line by walking into the store and ordering from a person. Maybe what we're really looking for when we pull into a drive-thru isn't speed. Maybe it's the opportunity to stay isolated, to stay in that little car world where everything is personalized just for us. Driving through means we're unlikely to visit a surrounding shop, because that would take more effort. It also means we're more likely to treat people like robots (after all, we're literally talking to them through robot-shaped boxes). Just ask a Starbucks barista which tip jar is more likely to be stolen — the one from the inside counter — pretty much never — or the one on the drive-thru window — once a month on average. (Source: my admittedly non-empirical evidence of talking to baristas.)

BORING, BORING BIG BOX BUILDINGS

Strip malls aren't designed for walkability; they're designed to streamline sales and to force our eyes to lock onto bright, colorful corporate marks. That's not a building; that's a logo. Strip malls can't really become part of our neighborhoods, either, since they usually aren't walkable and don't integrate with stand-alone shops, sidewalks or homes. They're designed for selling, not for living, and while there's nothing inherently wrong with that, I think we deserve better.

There are a lot of things I like about Birmingham, but one of them is how much people seem to rally around landmarks that are pegged for demolition. Old, faded signs are left on the sides of buildings instead of being painted over; an abandoned railroad across the street from my loft is being converted into a park; and when Pepsi covered up a favorite downtown marquis with a big soda billboard, the uproar was almost equivalent to the trash talk at a football game (quite a feat, considering the obsession with college football here).

Every six months or so (it seems), some corporation tries to bulldoze over an old landmark or a favorite local shop to put up a cookie-cutter big box store. There was the Starbucks that tried to shut down Lucy's Coffee & Tea by opening up next door; the Walgreens that would've leveled an old fire station and closed Bogue's Restaurant; the Chick-fil-A that wanted a drive-thru in the hippie-hangout that is Five Points. Follow your local city council or zoning commission, and you might be surprised how often corporately owned drugstore chains and fast food restaurants apply to demolish perfectly functional existing buildings, including historical landmarks, to replace them with homogenous corporate stores. What's worse? The new big boxes are often incredibly close to existing corporate stores that sell exactly the same products. It's an old joke that you can stand in the parking lot of a Starbucks and usually see another Starbucks, but isn't it just as silly that you can stand in the parking lot of a Walgreens and see a CVS?

A Walgreens across from a CVS (or vice versa) makes good corporate sense — you want to plant your flag where an existing store is thriving. The interloper hopes it can split the current tenant's sales and maybe drive them out of business. It's an easy way to tap into a market that already exists, and it's a clever way of getting your competitor's customers to consider your lower prices and better services, since they can actually see your billboards and window clings while standing in the other store. Competition in the marketplace can be a good thing, but this kind of corporate warfare is not. Prices may be slashed at both stores for awhile, but eventually something has to give, and either prices go back up and the neighborhood has two similar stores and no diversity of product offerings (decreasing the chances of walk-able shopping), or one store goes out of business and the neighborhood is left with an empty storefront. When corporations station their storefronts face-to-face like warring armadas, that's colonization, not community.

Even worse is when corporations use these same tactics on independent businesses. As much as I like Starbucks (when compared with other corporations), it's long been rumored that they plan sites for new stores by looking for thriving independents and opening up next door. I've heard Starbucks managers defend this practice, saying more coffee shops create a "coffee culture" that ends up being good for both stores. While it's true that Starbucks has done a lot to commercialize the coffee business in the U.S. and many independent coffeehouses benefit from the effects of that, it's a pretty big stretch to say opening next to a mom-and-pop is going to increase the indie's business. These predatory business practices are meant to build corporations and shareholder earnings, but they do that to the detriment of customers and communities.

Sometimes, they even do it to the detriment of

their own stores — different franchises from the same corporation can be victims of the parent company's dog-eat-dog interpretation of capitalism. The franchise is sort of a tricky entity when you're trying to shop small because they can vary so much in their corporate-ism. One franchise, like Little Professor bookstores, may be almost totally independent, circulating most money back into the community and only paying a small (less than $5,000) franchise fee to the parent corporation. But most franchises act as clever shadow entities for their parent companies, taking funding and tax breaks earmarked for entrepreneurs and sending them into their own conglomerates. McDonald's, Subway and Chick-fil-A are all franchises, meaning their owners are treated by the law much like independent shopkeepers, even though almost no important decisions are made locally, and a huge portion of tax money flows right back out of state to the parent company. Besides using them as a tax dodge, some corporations also pit franchises against each other, even allowing them as close as across the street. They let franchisees battle it out, effectively keeping profits low for both or chasing one owner out of the area. (Starbucks, by the way, does open stores close to each other, but is not franchised, so they're not an abuser in this case.)

Of course, the decisions of a parent company can

also hurt their franchisees. Chick-fil-A franchisees were stuck with the decisions of their founder, S. Truett Cathy, when his corporate donations made national news. And during the BP oil spill of 2011, many independent gas station owners who licensed the BP name were punished for the actions of their parent company. Big business wants us to believe that everything is going to keep getting bigger and better, and they put up buildings that are as big as our dreams of prosperity and success. But paying for a big building isn't the same as investing in community; big business isn't actually putting down roots in our cities and towns. A tree without roots isn't just badly nourished: It's also top-heavy, and when it falls, it's likely to take out anything in its path.

OIL SPILLS DON'T HAVE FEELINGS: WHY CORPORATIONS HURT COMMUNITIES

BP hurt more than just its licensed partners with its oil spill. The environmental damage affected all of us, and especially people who live in Gulf states. New

Orleans was hit particularly hard, having not yet recovered from Hurricane Katrina in 2005. After the oil spill, BP executives spent time lying and pointing fingers, and the company came off looking very bad. Really, though, their reaction made sense: A company that cares about people only for the profits they represent and invests in community only when it's profitable can't be reasonably expected to start caring when they do something wrong. BP had to pay for their screw up, but they didn't have to live with it because they don't live on the Gulf of Mexico. That limited their ability for compassion and, ultimately, for restitution as well. Owners of small shops, on the other hand, have to live where they work. When you actually live in a community, you typically aren't casual about putting it in danger.

Obviously, corporate abuse isn't unique to BP (I'm thinking of companies that give people diabetes, inflict cancerous chemicals on communities, destroy natural habits, spread E. coli because of poor sanitation, and sell cars with ignition problems, to list a few), but that company's actions in New Orleans make an interesting counterpoint to how local shopkeepers responded to Hurricane Katrina. That natural disaster wasn't the fault of any local business, but that didn't stop local merchants from stepping up to help rebuild the city. After the storm, even the few big boxes that took care of their employees and sent volunteers to help with cleanup opted to leave the city rather than reopen. Local shop owners, on the other hand, stayed to rebuild even after the news cameras had left (the city only recently reached its pre-hurricane population numbers), and they prioritized rebuilding their businesses to generate commerce in the city. As one New Orleans resident told me, "To corporate stores, we were just an insurance check. To local businesses, we were home." During tough times, big box stores hit the road in search for profits. Locally owned stores stay and help their communities heal.

The hugely negative impact of something like an oil spill is obvious, but corporations hurt our environment in less obvious ways every day: Big box stores take massive amounts of energy to heat and cool, especially when they're located in huge parking lots devoid of trees and plant life that would help regulate temperature. All the driving and flying and boating necessary to fill those huge shelves with products takes a massive amount of fossil fuel. And cyberstores that ship one or two products at a time create large amounts of waste from packaging instead of shipping items more efficiently in bulk like they would to a brick-and-mortar. Big box stores get their name from the boxy look of their buildings and from the huge boxes used to ship their goods. Small shops have a smaller environmental footprint and a smaller bite of the economic pie, but when it comes to stepping up and helping their communities, they leave some pretty big shoes to fill.

CEOs don't make the best decisions for neighborhoods, but it's not because they're evil or ruthless. It's because they're so far removed from the impact of their decisions that they make different choices than people who live in our communities. Sometimes that means building an ugly building because they're not the ones who have to drive by it every day. Sometimes it means creating corporate rules that stifle creativity, and sometimes it means trying to gloss over an oil spill with money and public relations (okay, that one's evil). We can't really expect chain stores to care about the declining quality of local schools or roads marked with potholes or underfunded parks that get more dangerous for kids, because although these things might be annoying (or worse) for those of us who have to live with them, they don't effect the bottom line on a national scale. Neither does giving to local charities — which is why small shops donate so much more to community causes than big box stores do.

Local business owners aren't always nice or fair or charming. Sometimes they give to charity for warm-and-fuzzy reasons, but even the selfish small business owners tend to donate more than their corporate counterparts. That's because a better community really can boost local business — a beautiful parks initiative, for example, doesn't put a blip in corporate numbers, but it can bring more business to the restaurant across the street from the park that goes from dangerous to inviting. Giving to local charities can also be a cheap way for small business owners to advertise, getting their names onto posters hung in other businesses around the city. Small businesses are more easily shamed if they say no to a local charity that solicits donations face-to-face, while franchisees and corporate store managers can hide behind their parent companies when they turn down a school or philanthropy looking for funding. And, while big box stores have to be careful about which charities they're supporting, sending donation-seekers through a labyrinth-like corporate vetting process so they don't inadvertently support an organization that conflicts with their company's message (i.e., if Starbucks funded a church mission trip and it turned out the money went to protesting homosexuality, going against the company's message of support for gay rights), smaller stores can more easily make donation decisions on a case-by-case basis without fear of reprisal from a parent company.

It's tempting to vilify corporations and exalt small shops, but it isn't really useful. Some corporate leaders are bad, and some are good. Some mom-and-pops look out for their communities, and some could care less. Because all stores, ultimately, are run by humans, there will always be outliers. But the corporate system makes doing good for the community very difficult — it's hard to automate, and it's hard to justify on a strictly profit-based scale. On the other hand, doing good for the community generally results in better PR and more profits for the smaller business. Statistically, small shops give back much, much more. Sometimes because they're good neighbors, and often because it makes good sense to do so.

CANDY CORN CATTLE RANCHERS: POISONING PEOPLE FOR PROFIT

One of the most massive examples of what happens when corporate greed overtakes human compassion is played out in the battle over our food supply. The drive for big profits drove corporations to replace our sugar with corn syrup and to pack our food full of chemicals and trans-fats that are literally killing us. Our health care system is buckling under the weight of, well, us — we're much too fat and we're dying because of it. This isn't a product of American gluttony; it's because of addiction.

We're addicted to our food (which is, arguably, not food at all) because what we're eating was designed by big business to be addictive — fat and sugar, even fake fat and sugar, make us want to eat more. We're dying because our food system is based on profits and subsidies instead of what's actually good for our bodies. The thing that gives us life has been perverted into something that's killing us. And it's business that's done this to us — with the help of a government that twisted capitalism into something that protected big companies over small ones instead of letting the free market run its natural course.

Our food culture is out of whack. You don't have to look at statistics to see that the nation is tending toward obesity — you just have to go to the mall or scroll through your Facebook feed. But if stats are your thing, you know that the numbers are staggering. More Americans than ever are dying of complications from being fat. More children than ever are diagnosed with Type 2 Diabetes. America is filled with food deserts — places of poverty in our own country where real food is so inaccessible that children can be fat and malnourished at the same time. They get calories, but they don't get nutrition. Their parents can't afford to buy or transport good food (try carrying food for four home on the bus), and at school they're fed substandard food like pizza and french fries. The way we eat, so central to our health and so important to our interaction with each other, is broken. This is capitalism at its worst, or at least its most hydrogenated.

We're just starting to realize that many of the things that we eat on a regular basis are, if not literally poisons, certainly not fuel for living like food should be. Take two of the biggest culprits, hydrogenated oils and high fructose corn syrup. These are finally being taken out of food because they've been flagged as dangerous. People are avoiding foods that contain hydrogenated oils and HFCS, and corporations are following the downward trend in their popularity and preemptively taking them out of foods that still contain them. But how did they come to be included in practically every pre-packaged food in the first place? Two reasons: These ingredients (and others like them) make food fast, and they make food cheap.

The Fruit Roll-Up is far superior to the fruit bowl — at least in terms of profit margin. Fruit Roll-Ups are stable, so they don't rot during shipping or when sitting on the shelf. Apples, on the other hand, spoil easily, can't be loaded efficiently into a truck (C'mon, apples! Why can't you be shaped more like a box!), and certainly can't hang out in the grocery store for several weeks if nobody buys them. Apples will spoil within weeks, but the Fruit Roll-Up can live to a grand old age, ready for the moment we choose to grab it. We want food to be cheap and convenient, and that means it needs to be efficient and long-lasting, making it through the sometimes months-long process of factory-to-table. It needs to be packaged, and it needs to be preserved.

Here's the thing about food: It doesn't keep that way naturally. Even dry beans or potatoes can't be exposed to temperature changes or prolonged light without spoiling or sprouting. And fresh fruit, like apples? Forget about it. You have to add stuff to food to make it last a long time on a shelf. The fact that these magic additives happen to be questionable chemicals didn't seem to register with the companies that injected them into our food supply.

Food that has a long shelf life tends to be bland by the time we eat it. To deal with a lack of taste, factories over-sugar and over-salt packaged food, and they add in a lot of fat to make it taste the way we like it. (Hydrogenated oil is a trans-fat, and HFCS is a super-concentrated sweetener.) When food is packed full of sodium, sugar and fat, it can sit on our shelves for a really long time before we eat it and still taste good, but loading food up with cane sugar or butter gets expensive. Cheap sugar and fat made in factories solves that problem: Hydrogenated oils and HFCS make food taste good even when it's really old and its nutrients are long gone, and they don't cost much money.

Why are these chemicals so cheap? It's partly because they're super-concentrated, so they pack a punch. Mostly, though, it's because our government manipulated their prices. See, Washington encouraged farmers to grow corn, and then they grew too much. Supply got too high, so then they manipulated corn prices, encouraging businesses to use corn. HFCS, a.k.a. High Fructose Corn Syrup, is a corn product (obviously), and it's cheap because corn is cheap — and cheap is very attractive to big business. This is also why the majority of our country's livestock are fed with corn, even though their bodies are designed to live on grass. Now that switch is effecting not only the cows' bodies, but our bodies as well when we eat beef. (Some farms have even fed their cows with candy, because it's even cheaper than corn. Since the candy's made with HFCS, these cows are literally fed with candy corn.) All that corn makes our diets homogenized, and that makes us unhealthy. It's part of what's making us fat, and it's happening so that our Twinkies will stay "good" on the shelf of the gas station until we pick them up and wrestle them out of their wrappers. It's happening because the government subsidized an industry and because we entrusted our food decisions to corporations. (Free market lovers, here's fuel for your fire — government subsidies gave us diabetes.)

Businesses do what's good for business, and saving

money on government-subsidized food additives is good for the bottom line. These corporations loaded food with sodium, HFCS and hydrogenated oils because the products sold better and cost less, so they posted better profits. They might not have known the total destructive toll this would have on society, but they knew it wasn't good for people. They did it anyway because it was good for shareholders, and those shareholders were probably not in the economic class that was eating McDonald's and Coke and GoGurt.

TOO MANY CROOKS IN THE KITCHEN

Fast food executives haven't been vilified as much as, say, tobacco executives, but in some circles they come close. To some extent, that's for good reason. Certainly they knew before the general public did that our food was dangerous. They had access to studies that at least suggested the dangers inherent in food, and the dangers were largely ignored. These companies don't care if kids are getting Type 2 Diabetes, because kids are not shareholders. It doesn't matter if your grandpa dies from complications resulting from obesity, because it doesn't cost them money. This view seems cynical (because it is cynical), but it's just how the system is inherently set up: The legal duty of a corporation is to make a profit for its shareholders, not to care about your health.

Did corporate executives know that they were selling unhealthy food? Probably. But turning them into punching bags kind of misses the point, which is that this problem exists not just because of corporate and governmental manipulation of the market. They might've served us food that was more addictive than we realized, but we compound the problem by continually choosing cheapness and convenience over anything else. That's what created the problem with our food supply, and that's what's causing a problem with our economy as a whole.

Food grown locally and in-season tastes much better than trucked-in produce and pre-packaged food (think about how fresh you'd feel after riding in a truck from California to the East Coast). Real food is better for our bodies (no artificial chemicals or colors, no HFCS or hydrogenated oils), and it's more nutritious. Growing food naturally or organically is a more environmentally sustainable way to farm, since it doesn't poison the soil (or the bees or the people). Less trucking of food means fewer greenhouse gases being released into the environment. And free-range livestock that are fed a natural diet are healthier for us to eat as meat.

THE LOCALIST

But it can be tough to adjust to eating this way. We have to relearn how to shop for food, how to cook our food, and sometimes how to eat. We have to learn to care for our food properly, how to not buy too much so it won't spoil and how to cook different things in a different way. We have to learn to make due with what's in season and understand what food labels mean. We have to be willing to ask questions, and to ask farmers about their growing methods. In some cases, we have to relearn how to taste.

The good news is, we are changing for the better. Many of us are making healthy food a priority, and we're creating a market for more organic food, more fresh food and more sustainable food. The slow food movement has a broad reach across the country, and that means new and better restaurants are cooking healthy food (and increasing demand even more). People are buying from neighborhood farmer's markets again; we're buying organic produce at the grocery; we're cooking at home more and grabbing fast food less. The way America eats is changing, and corporations are paying attention because we've made it profitable for them to do so. The market has spoken, and for once, it's speaking for us.

If we want continually better access to quality food, we'll have to pay for it, because healthy food is expensive. Maybe someday it won't be. Maybe someday demand and supply will come into better balance, and we'll overturn the laws that keep some food prices artificially low. For now, though, every time we shop at a farmer's market or choose locally grown food, we're on the front lines of the battle for our nation's food supply and for our local economies. In a way, it doesn't really matter if food producers are Bond villains — evil ne'er-do-wells intent on poisoning the populous — or if they're just slaves to our desires. Because no matter what, we can .007 this particular evil easily enough because we control the funding.

NEON JELLY BRACELETS, BIG HAIR, AND THE AMERICAN DREAM

I'm a child of the '80s, and as a kid, I really bought into everything the decade stood for — the commercialism and capitalism and neon, but also this crystallization of the American Dream: this sense that things could keep getting better and people would keep getting richer, and the only thing I had to do to be part of that success was to keep striving and fighting and working hard.

I started giving up on unlimited financial success a

few years ago for religious reasons (Jesus would've made a terrible stockbroker), but anyone who didn't have that same epiphany was forced out of their Reagan goggles anyway when our national — and global — economy collapsed. We haven't hit Depression and Dust Bowl levels of poverty, but we aren't doing so great, either. Lots of people lost their jobs and couldn't find new ones. Lots of people had to downsize and give up their houses and cars and dreams when their credit collapsed. Lots of people worked really hard and gave their bootstraps a really good tug and landed on the wrong side of a welfare line anyway.

News outlets love to broadcast about the financial meltdown, and bloggers like to write about how they're affected by it. Every generation seems to think it's got the best claim on being the worst treated by the economic collapse: The Greatest Generation saw their pensions and investments disappear. Baby Boomers expect to lose social security and say goodbye to early retirement. Generations X and Y can't advance in our jobs and don't know what to do if we lose them. And Millennials grew up expecting financial security that may never materialize. We all have valid reasons for feeling tricked. But maybe it's time we stopped feeling sorry for ourselves.

The financial collapse wasn't something most of us, regardless of generation, expected. But maybe we should have. Economic systems naturally rise and fall, and it's never wise to think their positive momentum will continue forever. For some reason, we all ignored that, and we set up our lives as if we'd only get more prosperous and hard times would never come and we'd become progressively richer and happier forever. We were living our lives like we were in an 80s music video, where the music was loud and the hair was big and the bad times would be as short as the skirts. It's a lot of fun to think that way. It's why I liked to think that way as a little kid.

But maybe it's time we grow up. Maybe we should admit to ourselves that life is full of ups *AND* downs and to start looking at prosperity, at least partially, as a chance to save up for hard times ahead. We've been trained to think growing up is the worst thing of all, but I'm thinking maybe it isn't. Acting like an adult can suck, but it can also be really exciting and freeing. It can also help us mature into people that we like being, developing personalities and economies that grow out of our choices instead of the choices that are made for us. Being less naïve and selfish with our finances and, instead, opening our eyes for the good of our community, and even our country, might just make our lives better, safer, and more of a stable place to land. Is creating that kind of world, that kind of economy, a lot of responsibility? Sure. But it could also be pretty incredible.

The things we dreamt about in the 80s aren't necessarily naïve or unreasonable (okay, maybe flying cars were). In general, it's okay to want prosperity for our country. It's okay to hope our government can provide for things like building interstates and defending us in a war. It's understandable to want good, safe neighborhoods for our kids to grow up in. And it's okay to be patriotic: to want a strong nation. But to do that, we need money in our budgets — both local and national. We need an economic system that rewards innovation and creativity. We need to understand what our money does, and how it can help.

It's no wonder we have a tough time grasping these issues of global finance and macroeconomics when we don't even have a clear understanding of microeconomics — or even of personal finance. We know how to spend money, but that's about where our comprehension ends. Most of us don't even see a real connection between how much we earn and how much we spend — hence our dependence on credit — so how can we be expected to have a grasp on higher economics and how they effect our communities, our states or our country? The good news is, these issues aren't really complicated; the math involved is pretty much on the elementary school level: The more money we give our local shops, the more we keep in our communities; and the more we give big box stores, the more we lose. The way we spend our money makes a difference. It's our right, and maybe our responsibility, to be sure we spend it well.

WHAT CAME FIRST, THE CHICKEN OR THE BOYCOTT?

Some families aren't allowed to talk about religion and politics at the dinner table, but in my house we weren't encouraged to talk about much else. (I'm guessing that's unsurprising if you've read this far.) We were like the Kennedys, if the Kennedys were working class Midwesterners who quoted Bible verses instead of philosophers. My dad felt that important subjects were the only ones worth talking about, so politics and religion were at the top of his conversation list. Dad might not be the most inoffensive choice for a dinner party invite, but he's right about one thing: At its root, politics is personal. Our laws and lawmakers effect real people every day, and the fact that we see politics as more of a sport or a circus is both a symptom of our political mess and part of the problem itself.

Maybe we can't stop corporations from becoming a part of our political process, but we can "vote" with our money when we agree or disagree with what they do. When we know a company treats its workers badly or supports a cause we're against, we have a responsibility to stop buying from them. Hobby Lobby and Chick-fil-A have a few things in common: They're both owned by Christians, they're both closed on Sundays, and they've both been boycotted in the last couple of years — not for closing on Sundays (although I've known some waffle fry devotees who've gone almost that far), but for putting money and company policy behind controversial political issues.

Hobby Lobby sued to win the right to avoid funding certain types of birth control (particularly the types which the company's leadership feel are not contraception but early abortion) for their employees. Chick-fil-A executives were shown to be funding organizations that created and distributed anti-gay propaganda. The Chick-fil-A story is so interesting not just because of the boycott that started when people found out that the nugget money was going toward "re-education," but also because of the "buy-cott" that sprung up in response when Chick-fil-A supporters headed to the fast food restaurant in droves to prove through purchasing that they supported Chick-fil-A and its chosen stance.

The issues at play in the Hobby Lobby and Chick-fil-A examples — abortion, contraception and gay rights

— are complex and polarizing. What's clear is, when we spend money at these businesses, we're supporting more than crochet supplies, glue guns and chicken biscuits. When we buy things we're putting money behind the causes the business supports. That means we have an obligation to use our purchasing power to support the things we believe in and to withhold our money from companies that we disagree with. Treating individuals (or corporations) who exercise their free speech differently is not the job of the government — but it is our job as citizens and as consumers. If you're pro-choice, it's hypocritical to buy yarn from Hobby Lobby, and if you support gay rights, it's best to learn to live without the waffle fries. That's how we exercise our free speech as individuals. That's how we send messages to the companies we do business with — in the language of money, the only language they understand.

This goes beyond companies who take religious or political stances. We can also financially punish companies that engage in deceptive practices, that treat their employees badly, that serve food they know is unhealthy. When we disagree, it makes sense to boycott a certain company and its parent corporation.

Sometimes, of course, this is easier said than done. It may not be practical (or even possible) to boycott huge companies like Kraft or Apple or to avoid repeat-offender

Monsanto. When we take stands like this, it can feel like we're throwing pebbles at a giant without even having a decent slingshot on our side. (All our slingshots are made of cheap plastic in China now, so they're not likely to stand up to a good giant-slaying anyway.) But this idea that our purchases don't matter is just a lie. Even the small spending is meaningful. Even the waffle fries make a difference. We may not be able to avoid buying from big box stores or from offensive corporations all of the time, but that doesn't mean that we shouldn't avoid buying from them when we know about their abuses. Big corporations have the power to destroy other people, to influence public policy, and to put local shops out of business only because we don't speak out against them, either with our speech or with our money. That silence is hurting us, and it's a problem we have the power to stop.

CORPORATIONS ARE(N'T) PEOPLE TOO: POLITICS, POWER AND PERSONHOOD

Some people say Americans have loud mouths. (By some people, I mean the rest of the world.) Freedom of speech is pretty important to us, and we exercise it often, both for big and important things like political debates and for silly things like blogging about the Kardashians. With few restrictions, we can pretty much say whatever we want. Ideally, we combine our freedom of speech with the responsibility to use it wisely, but even when we don't, we're still protected. Our liberty makes us annoying sometimes, but it also makes us powerful and free.

Unfortunately, our Supreme Court has cheapened our freedom of speech with a bad decision in the Citizens United case, allowing corporations to give money to political candidates in the name of free speech. This ruling manages to slap us twice, equating corporations with people and giving money the same considerations as speech. Now the battle for what's important about our humanity is being fought, not just in the corporate boardroom, but in the courtroom as well. Somehow, the same court that can't decide conclusively when a fetus becomes a person has decided to give Fortune 500 companies that title.

Treating corporations as people and money as speech is more than creepy. (Although it certainly is that — clearly, the justices don't read Science Fiction, or they'd know that personifying inanimate objects and monetary systems leads to some pretty nasty business.) Equating a business to a human life cheapens our humanity. This isn't just semantics: Elevating a business to the level of a person sends the message that corporate needs are just as important as a person's, and they certainly are not.

Corporations are not people. They don't breathe, love, create or feel. We should reject Citizens United not just because of common sense, but also because corporate decisions are made, not with reason, but with money. Publically traded corporations are legally obligated to report to and to produce profits for their shareholders. The system is rigged at its foundation to favor money above all, and a system like that shouldn't have a voice in our political process. Money may be the language that corporations speak, but equating it with actual, literal speech and giving it the same freedoms is dangerous. It sets us up to be a country where people who have wealth have more voice, are more likely to be listened to, and are more likely to be taken seriously. That's exactly the kind of country our founders escaped and tried to avoid becoming. We should not let the "we the people" that's so important and unique to us to be turned into "we, the Wal-Marts and the Microsofts and the Amazons."

When the government decided certain entities were too big to fail, they also made them seem too protected to be opposed by consumers. This led to an outpouring of rage known as the Occupy Wall Street movement, which saw people camping out for weeks in protest of big banks and big business. It's easy to see what attracted these protesters, and it's not just the Woodstock-like mix of anarchy, peace and love that seemed to develop through the weeks.

Our system, to put it mildly, is pretty messed up, and corporations gaining political influence without public transparency through the Political Action Committees protected by Citizens United is just the beginning: Big money strong-arms our political system to the point that our individual voices feel irrelevant, and banks and corporations are not held accountable for the laws they break or the lives they destroy. Corporations inexplicably avoid prosecution when they hire illegal and immigrant labor, but individual families of immigrants seeking the American dream are torn apart and punished for our demand for cheap products and cheap labor. And a nationwide Recession left almost every family struggling to get by.

On its own, shopping small won't solve our most com-plicated political problems, but it might bring us closer together as communities, and it's likely that unity would raise the current level of political discourse, creating a more civilized conversation that would help us find better solutions to our problems. Shopping locally would empower us and put more money into our local governments. It might just make us a more thoughtful people: a people who understand more about our communities. And that could put us in a better position for solving our problems and for building a better country.

The Citizens United ruling attacks America, it undermines what it means to be an American, and it chips away at our very humanity. But we can still make a stand, and we don't even need to hang out on sidewalks with picket signs to do it. Wall Street has our money because we give it to them, and that's something we can stop, or at least slow down, immediately. To really change Wall Street, we have to stop occupying Wal-Mart. With our money, we can tell businesses that being a person — a real one — still matters.

The restaurant industry says that fast food workers could soon be replaced by robots. Unfortunately, even robots can't live on minimum wage.

—Stephen Colbert
The Colbert Report

****

THE AUTOBOT NEXT DOOR:

The Human Cost of Our Drive for Profits

****

CREATIVITY IS LIFE

When I was a little girl, I had regular chores (cleaning my room, etc.), and I also had creativity chores. My parents would put out a pile of magazines and tell my sister and I to make collages out of the images, or cut shapes out of cardboard and have us make designs by tracing them onto paper, or give us instructions to make designs out of our names by the time they got home from work. None of the assignments were particularly difficult, and none of them were especially productive by normal standards. But they were still important, because they taught us to think creatively and to problem solve. They gave us a connection to creation and to our work. They taught us that our work has meaning not just because of our productive output or our contribution to society (although that's part of it), but to our souls as well. It's why children play with crayons and Play Dough and construction paper instead of just learning conceptually. It's why we're attracted to hands-on hobbies like cooking and rebuilding cars and knitting. Creating something means that we matter. It makes us human. It makes us happy.

This spirit of creation and innovation is also important to who we are as Americans. We prize invention, and we like to imagine ourselves as a society that cultivates creativity and welcomes new ideas. We're the country that invented electricity and the telephone and the Internet. Heck, our entire country was created not 250 years ago out of the dream of a few people wanting to escape being controlled, setting out to start something totally new and building a different system of government that would end up changing the world from a few words on paper. We are a people who value the go-getter, the innovator, the builder and the job creator.

But on a day-to-day basis most of us aren't entrepreneurs or inventors. We're employees and subordinates, and we don't think our choices matter — this makes us feel passive and inauthentic. Most of us don't make anything, and most of what we buy is distributed and produced by machine. Efficiency is now valued above imagination, and we feel like hypocrites when we see how far our lives are from the qualities we prize most. We don't produce things that we love. We aren't fulfilled. We don't see ourselves as creators — we're consumers.

We shame ourselves with this kind of thinking, and it's a lie. As my coworker Cal says, "We create something with our purchases. Why wouldn't you want to create something beautiful?" We've become so detached from our spending habits that we don't think our actions have real impact. We've forgotten that the money we spend actually has the power to build the neighborhoods we want to live in and to strengthen our communities. Because purchasing ultimately builds things, it's a creative act, but that doesn't mean that we necessarily like what we're creating.

When we buy without thinking about the results of our spending, we take power away from communities and give it to corporations. We fund ugly big box stores instead of parks, and we keep money out of our tax system where it could go toward education. To fix this, we can't just pretend it's not happening. When Dr. Frankenstein abandoned his monster, convinced that turning his back would absolve him of responsibility for what he'd made, he only made the problem worse. Our creation might be an economy that revolves around profit instead of people, and not a beast who walks the streets of London, but the lesson is the same. (And a green, destructive monster with bolts in its neck that lacks the capacity to love isn't such a bad metaphor for our economy, come to think of it.)

Instead of ignoring the damage our purchases are making, we could start making them count. Corporate interests try to convince us that our choices don't matter, that our money is just a drop in the bucket, and that wise decisions aren't worth making. They've taken our power to create away from us, but we can get it back, and in some areas we're already starting to. We all have access to more local and more organic food than we had ten years ago because we've created change through purchasing, and we've created a market for hybrid vehicles like the Prius by insisting car companies provide us with better options and supporting those options with our purchases. Some communities are already embracing localism, rejecting corporations that want to move in, and supporting independents instead.

We can build better economies, better communities, and better products. Anyone who tells us we can't, whether it's a politician or a corporation, is lying. When we own up to our role as creators of our communities, as artists who paint more life into our neighborhoods with each dollar we spend, we take back the power to change

WANT SUCCESS AT A BIG BOX? DON'T THINK OUT-OF-THE-BOX

Small shops tend to promote individuality more because it makes financial sense for them: Local stores thrive off of individuality, expert knowledge and unusually personal customer service, and without a system in place to cheaply train new employees (like big corporations have), it's usually less expensive for a local store to promote and reward good employees than to replace them with new, untrained people. When we buy locally, we reward this kind of system, and we are voting for humanity instead of for the stripping away of validation and personality. Corporations, on the other hand, tend to crush individuality as part of their design.

Corporations thrive on conformity. Generally speaking, they can't make the broad-sweeping decisions or get the big-number buying power that keeps prices low if decisions are made at the individual level. Responding to the needs of one community is too taxing to make economic sense, and changing or waiving policy for one individual is even more costly. Big box stores work by creating a mold and making cookie-cutter copies of the same thing over and over. That way, mistakes can be eliminated (or at least reduced), work isn't duplicated, and the success profile of one store can be used again and again.

In the best of times, this system works. Standardized logos and colors make brands identifiable to consumers and mean new stores don't have to prove themselves after opening because they're already aligned with a powerful brand. Employees follow guidelines of behavior so HR departments are kept small and not duplicated on the local level. The corporate system avoids a lot of waste.

Unfortunately, individuality is the baby in this bathwater, and people are stripped of the very things that make us human. Like the buildings that it erects in its own corporate image, a big box store usually expects its employees to fit into a specific corporate mold as well. Employees that don't fit the status quo often don't advance, if they're even accepted in the first place. Sometimes this means tattoos and piercings are off the table, but too often things like being a woman or being black can get you skipped over by recruiters or for promotions at a big box store. In a system where the people in charge of promoting are rarely the people who work with you on a day-to-day basis, the qualities that get you promoted, and the qualities that disqualify you, are skewed. Certain personality types are favored over others, even if they're not best suited for the jobs being considered.

At many retail businesses, you'll have to take a personality test before you're hired. It's supposed to determine whether or not you're the kind of person who might steal. If you fail this test, you won't be hired. Not because you've done anything wrong, but because a corporation has labeled your personality as dangerous. It's like the movie Minority Report, where people are punished for crimes they haven't committed, except with fewer hot tubs full of creepy psychics. This practice, in a way, is even creepier, because it's already happening. Along with potential thieves, these tests weed out deep thinkers and out-of-the-box personalities who could be the best problem solvers or the most empathetic leaders, because admitting that you understand the motivation to steal, even if you don't condone it, results in failure. Forget innocent until proven guilty — these tests punish known innocents just for not fitting into a corporate mold.

Even if you make it past the personality-control test and get a job, odds are you won't be rewarded for the good behavior you were tested for, because it's cheaper for big box stores to create constant turnover than to reward employees for good sales or good teamwork. If they retain employees, they'll eventually need to promote them, paying more for the same people and providing them with benefits. That gets expensive, and it's cheaper to punish employees for arbitrary infractions and refuse to honor hard work. People who post great sales still have their hours cut and exemplary performance reviews are discouraged. (If the parent company decides to cut costs, they can use this record of infractions as a weapon to slash labor, because a company isn't penalized for un-employment claims if it can show a record of corrections as justification for termination.)

This system is perfectly legal, but it's not ethical, and it certainly doesn't create the kind of work force our country needs to be strong and rebuild our econo-my. Having a livable job as a pawn in the chess game that is corporate America is possible, but it depends a lot on having a good manager (and remember, creepy personality tests have rejected the empathetic ones) and flying under the radar of bosses who make decisions for you without ever seeing your face. The corporate big box system is set up to discourage personal fulfillment. It rewards robots and time-savers, not human beings.

Training a work force to behave this way and rewarding them for it is un-American, both in concept, because we're a country that traditionally prizes out-of-the-box thinking and individual leadership, and in practice, because a work force full of people trained to act like sheep is unlikely to result in the kind of entrepreneurship and innovation that could increase GDP. More importantly, treating people as if their personalities are inconveniences that need to be snuffed out so they can behave more like corporate robots is inhuman and inexcusable.

There are quiet abuses, like randomly cracking down on employees for not upholding arbitrary corporate policies, denying health care to part-time workers (almost every major big box company does this — Starbucks and Whole Foods being notable exceptions), shorting employee paychecks in order to keep their hours under the full-time mark (this is illegal, but it's a common practice), requiring unreasonably short lunch breaks, recording poor performance reviews even for outstanding performance in order to protect the company in case of potential lawsuits, and treating employees like thieves by permitting or even requiring bag searches (some retail stores, like Urban Outfitters, search employees whenever they set foot in the store, even when they're not on the clock). Whistleblowers against corporate abuse from store managers are routinely disbelieved, punished or stuck in a corporate appeals system, and accusations that are supposed to be kept secret rarely are.

In my experience, often the best salespeople, the kindest coworkers, and the most effective company advocates are the very people who are fired from corporations because someone behind a computer at headquarters doesn't interpret facts correctly or because the employee doesn't fit the status quo. You can be a fantastic salesperson, a hit with customers, a real benefit to your store and to your corporation, and even a high earner, and that won't keep your corporate job safe. Increasingly, the only way to ensure job security is not to be good at your job, but to know how to play the corporate game and how to tell corporate what it wants to hear. This goes beyond asking employees to behave a certain way at work and puts individualism and critical thought in the crosshairs.

A PENNY SAVED IS AN EMPLOYEE BURNED

Even at the best of times, food service and retail work are not enviable jobs. Dealing with the paying public is difficult — for every kind customer, you have five angry ones who take out their problems on you (even, and maybe especially, when they have nothing to do with you). It's an easy way to lose your faith in humanity, and that's before you even get to job perks like cleaning bathrooms, wearing hairnets, smelling like grease or spoiled milk all the time, and watching your hands shrivel away due to constant exposure to sanitation chemicals. But those are just parts of the job, and they can be made bearable, and sometimes even fun, by taking pride in your work and finding camaraderie with your coworkers the way you often can at an independently owned store or at a corporation with an especially good manager. The kinds of jobs lots of people consider low-level can actually be quite fulfilling and enjoyable in the right situation. Unfortunately, the corporate model doesn't foster that kind of situation because keeping low-wage earners unhappy and unmotivated is better for the bottom line than keeping them around and having to compensate them for long-term service.

The most effective way to keep prices low, of course, is to pay your work force as little as possible. In most retail and service businesses, labor is one of the highest expenses, so it pays to manipulate your employees into accepting lower wages and giving up benefits like health care and retirement savings programs. There are the day-to-day low salaries and employee cuts that we're used to seeing from big box stores, but there are plenty of other abuses that go far beyond those. Wal-Mart, for example, has been accused of locking their employees inside stores overnight so they can't leave, and of discrimi-nating against women as a matter of policy. The same accusations have surfaced so often that it seems clear they're indicative of business-as-usual and not just the decisions of a few bad managers, as the company would like us to believe.

The low wage at most corporately owned stores is keeping our country in recession and putting an unsus-tainable drain on federal resources, but it's routinely misrepresented by political talking heads and ignored by wealthy and middle class people who believe hard work always leads to prosperity despite facts that say other-wise. As a white, over-educated, middle-class person, I know a lot of other white, over-educated, middle-class people. We like to do things like eat hummus, buy records on vinyl, and start book clubs because those are the kinds of things over-privileged white kids do. In one of these book clubs, we read *NICKLED AND DIMED*, an excellent book detailing the struggles of the working poor. There's a passage in the book that describes eating peanut butter sandwiches for every meal when you can't afford proper food, and one of the girls in the club latched onto that as proof that being poor in America isn't that hard. "I ate peanut butter sandwiches all through college, and I didn't mind it," she said between sips of red wine.

I'd gone to college with this girl, so I happen to know she was never without a meal plan that covered three meals a day, and I doubt she's ever had peanut butter sandwiches for two meals in a row, let alone two months. Still, she honestly believed that, because she ate a PB&J once, she understands what it's like to live off of them almost exclusively for weeks. In a way, she's right — peanut butter doesn't rank high on the list of problems with American poverty. Much worse is the fact that minimum wage workers lack a livable income, access to education, and sometimes to health care. (Obamacare changed the healthcare piece somewhat, but in states like Alabama, the truly poor still don't have access to affordable medical care.)

A lot of us push aside the concerns of the American poor. After all, most of us in the middle class had to work less-than-ideal jobs on the way up the corporate ladder or while we figured out what to do with our lives. What we don't take into consideration is that we had these jobs when we were young, single, healthy, and had futures full of possibility. It's different to hold these positions when you're an adult with a family and an older body more prone to disease and exhaustion, and when you lack the financial or educational wherewithal to change your life. While it's true that minimum wage workers may not be suffering as much as, say, starving children in third-world countries, and their work is not always back-breaking, the toll minimum wage, big-box work takes on a person's humanity is large and shouldn't be ignored. It's hard to be treated like a machine all day, to do work that isn't noticed or rewarded, and to realize that you barely matter to your company's leaders. And it's hard to be constantly mistreated by customers, treated like a robot, and punished for the decisions of a parent company that you have no control over.

Disrespectful treatment and low wages aren't just bad for people; punishing our workforce like this is bad for our economy, too: The costs that big companies save by not paying living wages are passed onto us as taxpayers. Our country is flooded with out-of-work people, including hard workers, skilled workers, and even plenty of veterans who serve our country well and come home to unemployment (or to underpaid and unfulfilling employment). When low-wage workers can't pay rent, they go on welfare, and we pay for that. When they don't make enough to buy food, we pay for their food stamps. When they can't afford health care, we pay for their emergency room visits. McDonald's can do business the way they do only because we the taxpayers supplement their salaries. Why are McNuggets and Fish Fillets so cheap? Because we're subsidizing their supersizing with every tax return.

Minimum wage workers are so underpaid that they can't make ends meet. They're living off sandwiches, but they're also accruing debt for basic food and medical needs. When they fight back, they're met with resistance and the threat of lost jobs. Fast food workers are recently organizing and protesting their low wages, but the companies that employ them say raising wages would result in lost business and require job cuts as a result. For a company like McDonald's that makes its money almost solely based on low cost of food instead of on quality, that might be right. If McDonald's raises wages, they probably will have to raise prices, and that will cost them customers. But is that such a bad thing? McDonald's will probably never make the choice to take care of their employees, but we can choose not to support a company whose entire business model is based on mistreating people. Maybe dollar hamburgers and boxed apple pies aren't worth that.

But even when a community tries to reject subsidizing a corporation, they usually can't. In 2013, Washington DC tried to legislate better pay for workers at a proposed Wal-Mart. Instead of changing policy, Wal-Mart blamed the district for punishing job creation, ignoring the fact that the quality of those jobs was so low that the benefit was negligible. In the end, Wal-Mart escaped paying the higher wage. Those costs didn't go away — they were passed to the community instead of the corporation. That's not good business, and it isn't capitalism. It's corporate greed and government failure.

OUT OF SIGHT, OUT OF MIND

It's not just retail workers and food service workers who pay a cost for our convenience when we shop big-box. They might be eating peanut butter while we eat cake (so to speak), but there are even more dramatic abuses happening where we can't see them. If we could see inside the warehouses that fulfill our online shopping orders, for example, we'd see Americans putting in long hours of tough physical labor with notoriously bad, and sometimes nonexistent, health benefits.

But at least in the U.S., workers are somewhat protected by labor laws. The most horrible abuses happen overseas, where labor is cheapest and where we're least likely to care about working conditions. In order to keep prices low on many of our products (especially electronics), corporations search outside the country both for labor and for tax havens. Doing business offshore helps companies avoid paying taxes, but it also allows them to pay little to nothing for labor and to allow the most callous abuses of the people who make our stuff.

Workers in some overseas factories are tricked into committing to long-term contracts that amount to servitude. They're physically and emotionally mistreated as a rule. Some have to live at the factories so there's no escape, even at the end of the day. Many of the people who make our iPhones and flatscreen TVs are so miserable, underpaid, and have so little chance for escape that factories see rates of suicide far above what's normal.

Our computers and toys are cheap because people go without food, without their families, and without a hope for the future. We can enjoy Black Friday and tax-free shopping holidays because human beings are locked in warehouses with no access to the outdoors. Overseas labor does more than cut American jobs (although it does do that). It makes people into slaves who don't have access to basic first aid or emergency care, even though they're put in dangerous positions by their jobs every day. These tragedies — that's the only accurate way to describe them — are easy to ignore because we can't see them. But that doesn't make ignoring them the right thing to do. When we buy corporately instead of buying local, we're supporting the companies that push man-ufacturing overseas and use flashy packaging and low prices to distract us from inexcusable abuse.

If we have the power to change the system through our purchases, why do we feel so powerless? Why does it feel like any efforts we make, especially by choosing local buying over corporate purchases, are just a drop in the proverbial bucket? Part of this is because our world is so connected now, and our concerns, news stories and cultural trends are increasingly international. Global con-nectivity is in many ways wonderful, but it's also served to make us feel insignificant. It may be "a small world after all," but it just feels like an overwhelming one. We feel jerked around by everything we "need" to see and buy, swung onto the next big thing before we have time to process what's in front of us.

Big companies benefit from this feeling. If we don't think our choices have any impact beyond ourselves, than why not make choices purely based on what we want and how cheaply we can get it? This gives corporations the excuse they want to cut wages and treat people inhumanely. It allows them to cut corners and make cheap products that fall apart in months instead of years and to manipulate the political system with lobbyists and big financial donations. It lets them justify cutthroat tactics that destroy other companies and other people in the interest of making stuff cheaper. We don't call them to task — not because we don't care, but because we don't think we matter.

Our switch to overseas labor is partly due to advances in tech that rely mostly on foreign factory prices, but also to a clamoring for discounts due to a worldwide financial collapse and American recession. We've long had an obsession with cheapness: with finding a deal or getting a steal. But now that so many people are out of work and can't even afford to put food on the table, much less pay rent, low prices are more than a luxury — they seem necessary to make ends meet. And for those of us not in financial distress, the loss of a job or a drastic cut in salary seems so close that it has us working longer hours and stressing more over every dollar.

The trouble is, buying from corporations extends our recession. Big box stores may be cheaper in the short run, but they send even more jobs and money out of the country. Buying locally puts more people back to work and puts more money into our local communities where it can serve those who are unemployed (and help their families).

The good news is that our financial system can change faster than we imagine. The same globalism and Internet connectivity that's led to cheap labor and mistreatment of foreign workers also makes it easier to support our local shops. We can use search engines and social media to discover more independents, to find out what they have to offer, and to share our small successes with our friends and neighbors. Our buying decisions put real money back into our communities in real numbers, not just in fractions. The truth is: We do matter. We are creative people, and we can create the change we want to see in our economy, in our communities, and in our lives.

SINGLE-SERVING LIFE

Shopping small helps us lean in to our humanity. That's more than just a metaphor: When we spend money at locally owned stores, a lot more of it stays inside our communities and inside our country, recirculating so that our money builds and shapes the communities we live in even after we spend it. We already know that each dollar we spend in a local shop helps that individual shop, but it also has a wider impact, funding roads and schools and community projects instead of leaving the state or the country. But shopping locally also has a more personal impact, forcing us to think about other people, to break our established patterns, problem-solve, and limit our endless consumption by combining shopping trips and practicing patience by waiting until later even for the things we want right now. It's an antidote for the depersonalization that happens when we shop online and at big box stores, choices that feed the desire for speed and individualized selection that come with our quick-fix digital lifestyles.

Trying to stop technology is a bit of a fool's game, but holding onto our humanity during its advancement is not. We can't and shouldn't prevent the future of digital technology, but we can create a world where technology serves human and communal interests. As our devices get faster and more connected, it's important that we prioritize each other and hold onto the things that make us human. That means putting love over "likes." It means sometimes stopping to enjoy a conversation or a meal instead of Instagramming it. The digital obsession with speed and connectivity has a profound impact not just on our devices, but on the way we think and live and love each other. Technological advancements are fantastic, but not at the expense of our spirituality, our emotional health, our creativity, or our economy.

Technology has made individualized, single-serving lives possible for all of us. We're constantly communicating with each other through social media, but we feel more disconnected than ever as we replace real connection with frequent updates and virtual likes. Our world can seem more like a sci-fi novel than reality: I carry a tablet that holds an entire library, but it's lighter than a paperback book. I have a personalized device that acts as a real-time communicator with family and friends, that plays me songs and movies and talks back to me and predicts the weather. That's all pretty great, but it doesn't make me happy. Siri can give me directions, and she might even tell me a joke, but she won't give me the insight of a real conversation. She's not passionate or funny or surprising, and she's never once given me a hug.

This kind of isolation once seemed attractive to me; I used to think it would be really cool to be agoraphobic. I'd sit in my little apartment, safe from the outside world, working behind a desk for coworkers I never saw. I'd get food delivered and I'd live my life mostly through TV. Hiding from the world and watching television was pretty much all I ever wanted to do anyway, so this seemed like a lovely and restful life. That dream is very much within my reach as an adult — I could work remotely, and pretty much every product I'd wish for could be delivered to my door. Now, though, I realize that isolation isn't all that great, even with all the snacks and entertainment I could ever want. Being completely alone, existing apart from community, just doesn't make me healthy or happy.

This move away from sentiment and toward efficiency and commercialization and its effect on humanity isn't really anything new. The Industrial Revolution dragged us into the modern era on the backs of the working class: breaking up families, plunging people into poverty, and clearing the way for rampant disease and air pollution, not to mention fire and crime. I wouldn't want to go back in time and prevent the Industrial Revolution (for one thing, the DeLorean and flux capacitor I'd need to go back would cease to exist once I changed the past), and I wouldn't choose to give up my devices or undo the digital revolution, either. But embracing change doesn't mean accepting it at any cost. We must find a way to allow our humanity to thrive even as technology advances. Buying locally encourages real, personal connection in a daily way. Putting money into our local economies strengthens our communities, creating a foundation for building better friendships, better families, and more of the person-to-person connection that we need to survive as humans.

I AM NOT MY METADATA

Computers and algorithms now make it possible to "have it our way" even when we're completely isolated, giving us thousands of recommendations based on our buying data with just a couple of keystrokes. These cyber-choices do a good job with obvious purchases, but they break down when the question becomes more complicated. An algorithm can't help us if we have unpredictable tastes or opinions, because it's set up to make choices based on probability and metadata instead of personality. Book recommendations from Amazon, for example, break down quickly when we input popular authors (it just recommends more of their books) or books in a series (it selects more books in the same series).

Beyond the logistical limitations of computer-generated recommendations, they're also calculated to put the needs of the corporation above those of the consumer. Netflix might show you movies similar to the ones you like, but it won't help you find a movie it doesn't carry, even if you might love it. Amazon's reviews are generated

partly by which publishers pay to promote their books, so
you're really getting advertising, not an impartial review.
They can't recommend something based on your personality and sense of humor, because a computer can't
calculate those things. Metadata is really cool and can
do some amazing things, but it's still not as sensitive as
the human soul.

It's not just computer recommendations that push
corporate agendas — even the human staff at big box
stores are forced to push certain seasonal products
and company promotions (like store credit cards) on
their customers. Local shops see individual choice as
valuable, while most corporations see it as a hurdle
to be overcome: Corporations pay big money for trend
forecasting to try to be ahead of the game on what's
new and popular. They have to make these educated
guesses early in order to get entire production schedules
and sales teams in line in time for the product launch.
They have to prepare for every oversight, every out of
stock store, every eventuality in every franchise. That
means they have to require their staffs to promote these
seasonal products when they do come out, or they'll be
stuck with huge amounts of stock that has to be liqui-
dated because it didn't move. Small shops, on the other
hand, can respond to market trends in ways the big guys
can't because they can react to specific community or

neighborhood tastes without being burdened by corporate red tape. They're less likely to force trends on customers, since they can experiment with micro-trends and niche markets before sinking big money into their strategies. Indies can respond to customer choice instead of trying to manipulate customers into buying what corporate interests have already decided on.

Local shops prioritize giving solid feedback and recommendations, and they'll usually even send you to a competitor if they can't give you what you're looking for. It sounds counter-intuitive, but a lot of small shops are okay with watching you walk out their doors once if it means connecting you with the right product in hopes that you'll be loyal to them in the long run because you trust their advice. Most staff at independents have chosen their jobs because they truly enjoy what they're selling, and that makes them far more honest about which products last and which are a waste of money. Amazon will still have your business if it makes a bad recommendation, but an independent probably won't. Local shops know this, so they're usually willing to lose a sale if it means winning a customer.

Sure, there's always the possibility that we'll get outstanding service from a clerk at Best Buy, a barista at Starbucks or a bookseller at Barnes and Noble, but great customer service at big box stores is the exception, while at small shops it's the rule. That personal connection puts better and more tailored products in our hands, and those sales reward the companies that make quality goods, paving the way for less junk and more quality manufacturing.

This isn't just about movie recommendations and book reviews. Owners and employees at small shops have to live with the results of their actions every day, and their decisions are often different — more humane and more compassionate — because of it. If the decision-makers at the corporations that made our packaged food actually had to meet and talk to people getting fat, developing diabetes and dying from food-related illnesses, they might've made different decisions about what went into their products. If oil company presidents lived on the coast, they might've been more cautious about drilling and more serious about preventing spills. And if executives at Wal-Mart and Amazon had to live with the human costs of poverty, they might not be so cavalier about prioritizing profits over people.

Far from encouraging creativity, most corporations try to shut down any advances that don't directly profit their shareholders. The corporate tendencies to buy up the competition and to sue, trademark and patent their way into monopolizing entire industries is bad for innovation and diversification of products. Instead of encouraging

new businesses and ideas that could promote progress
in the U.S. and the world, and instead of putting more
wealth into our individual communities and creating
more jobs, businesses with a myopic focus on profit
shape our communities into machines meant to pump
dollars into overseas markets.

Local businesses, in contrast, are effective drivers of
innovation and niche products. This isn't because owners
of mom-and-pops are really any better or worse than
corporate CEOs — no business, not even a local business, has pure and altruistic motives. But the independent model is better for our communities because, when
we shop small, we buy from a broad variety of stores
and shops instead of from just one entity. That means
lots of decisions and lots of players — all of whom have
voices that matter, and none of whom can control an
entire industry on a corporate whim. More voices in
the decision-making process mean more energy, more
ideas and more solutions. It means more innovation and
more unique thinking. Prioritizing local shopping can be
difficult, but putting small shops first means creating an
economy where creativity is embraced.

HAVING IT OUR WAY KIND OF SUCKS

Our ability to communicate with each other has atrophied to the point that shopping locally can be uncomfortable because it requires connecting with another person. But the thing that's so hard about small shopping is also what makes it so essential. You have to look your salesperson in the eyes — and they do the same. They see you as a person, as a neighbor, and they're more likely to care about you because of that. It may not mean they'll become a personal friend or bend over backwards to help you every time (although it often does mean that), but it will make your shopping experience more tailored to your needs. A human being will always care more about you than your computer does, and when we're viewed as people instead of as data and decimals, we get better service in the long run.

Shopping locally helps us connect in a literal way, and it helps us improve the quality of life in our communities by giving them the money they need to flourish. We need to learn each other's names, to care for each other, in order to grow as individuals and stay healthy. That's how we improve our communities, how we work better as teams and innovate more, and how we bring more money into our communities. We've come to experience this kind of intimate bonding as inappropriate or dangerous, when it's actually essential. So much of our lives are centered on consumption, and so much of our time is spent in front of screens. We miss the opportunity to look into each other's eyes, to touch other people, to have even short conversations. We've been ignorant to the fact that always choosing the easiest, quickest way might be hurting us, but ignorance is not bliss (numbness, maybe).

Americans have a reputation: We want what we want when we want it. You can see it in our slogans, like Burger King's "Have it your way." You can see it in our 24-hour restaurants and our personalized Netflix queues. There's something awesome about this, but there's also something missing in our lives. Our quick-return, single-serving, big-box lifestyle is giving us exactly what we want, but it's not making us happy. As it turns out, living in community is essential to our humanity, and without it we feel disconnected, our actions seem impotent, and our lives feel meaningless. No matter how we look at it, spiritually ("love your neighbor as yourself" in one form or another is key in most religions) or scientifically (packs and tribes have been essential to our development as a species), we're happier and healthier people when we connect with each other. Everything from scientific journals to Simon and Garfunkel note that living in isolation is not so good for us. No man is an island, and the man who tries to live like one does damage to his soul.

Capitalism: God's way of determining who is smart and who is poor.

—Ron Swanson
Parks & Rec

CHAPTER FIVE

****

SELLING OUR SOULS:

Is Small Shopping a Matter of Faith?

****

LOVE AND LEFTOVERS

In our bank statements, all those purchases we forget about, all those things we rationalize, are laid bare. What we spend on ourselves compared to what we spend on other people is written down in black and white without the benefit of our excuses. Where we spend our money shows who we are and what we value. It effects change in our environments and communities. It connects us to our neighbors. We help each other, and we help the poor. We realize that our own needs are not more important than the needs of others.

To me, this makes buying locally a profoundly spiritual act: a blow against the consumerist culture that we live in that makes it difficult to take actions that are helpful or holy. The more time I spent thinking about shopping locally, and the more I thought about why it matters so much to me, the more I was forced to evaluate my core belief system. Maybe it's not immediately obvious why I'd include a chapter about faith in a book about shopping. We like to pretend that religion is somehow above financial concerns, that spirituality is more ethereal — separation of church and bank, so to speak. The truth is, for better or for worse, money effects almost every aspect of our lives and our communities, and that includes spirituality.

Money matters to our systems of morality, because it matters to our lives. That doesn't really depend on which religion we practice, or even if we're not religious at all: Muslims, Jews and Christians alike are called to serve the poor. Hindus believe that how we treat others is so important that it determines our place in the next life and that souls are to be honored even when they've passed out of human form. Buddhists honor the life force of every being and attempt to rid themselves of desire and consumerism. Atheists and humanists believe we cease to exist when we die, making the quality of the lives we have even more important. Morality, and in particular religion, requires sacrifice. It asks us to be honest with ourselves, to examine our motivations, and to act out our beliefs in our communities as well as in our souls.

As we've been talking about throughout the book, when we buy big box, we usually get things cheaper. That's because they're made more cheaply, and that often means the people who made and sold those things were mistreated. When we pay less than something should cost, someone's paying for it. We take advantage of the disenfranchised all over the world to get more toys, clothes and computers for ourselves. When we decide not to care for the poor (and instead of pulling them up, we walk over them for the sake of cheaper Xboxes), I can't help but think that will reflect poorly on us from an eternal perspective.

Money reveals who we are and what's important to us. When I started blogging about shopping locally (and before that, personal finance), I had to really look at my credit card and debit card statements, and they showed almost to the exact percentage what I really valued in life. I saw a pop of spending in the hours after getting bad news at work. I tended to stress-eat ranch fries at fast food restaurants, and that pain showed up in black-and-white on my bank statements. It wasn't all bad news — I saw money I lent to friends or gave to charity and food I bought for a coworker who was going through a hard time. Even the gaps in my spending were revealing, proving that I went to a park instead of the movies, or read a book instead of escaping to the mall.

When I think of buying locally, I think of love stories and leftovers. (Uh ... just go with me for a minute.) Anyone who doesn't think leftovers are romantic hasn't heard the story of Boaz and Ruth from the Torah. He was a rich landowner. She was a poor widow. He told his men to leave the leftover wheat in the field so the poor could come and get something to eat. Boaz saw Ruth picking up some wheat sheaves (or whatever), and the rest is history. Caring for the poor worked out pretty nicely for

Boaz, who got a hot new wife (and got to be part of the line of Christ in the bargain), but this leftovers idea wasn't original to him. It's a Jewish custom to always leave extras along the edges to care for and remember the poor. That's actually one theory as to why orthodox Jewish men grow out their sidelocks — it's a daily reminder to always leave extra at the edges for those who don't have enough.

Shopping local is my sidelocks. This everyday action is a constant reminder to me to think of others, to prioritize community, and to be sure that my actions take care of others instead of hurting them. It's true that shopping small does have a real impact on the community, but it's also true that, in my life, the reminder that my actions have meaning for others is just as important. We need daily reminders to remember the poor because caring for people in need is so easy to forget.

FAITH, INCORPORATED

Most of us who profess faith in a higher power assume God requires some kind of sacrifice from us: Two of the five pillars of Islam, zakat and sawm, involve self-sacrifice. Buddhists attempt to rid themselves of their own egos. The Hindu tradition includes ritual sacrifice, as does the teachings of the Jews, who are called to sacrifice all sorts of stuff: animals, first-born sons, foreskins, etc. And Christian scriptures tell us that everything belongs to God, and that we don't own our possessions or our money, but are merely guardians, or stewards, of those things.

In the U.S we use religion for everything from marketing to politics, but we seem to have lost sight of the sacrificial parts. Family values are a huge talking point for us, but there's not much discussion about the much more religious concept of community. Modern evangelical Christianity tells us to focus on the family, but Jesus didn't say that. He actually said the opposite ("Who are my brothers and sisters? All who follow me."), and he never ever chose the wealthy over the poor. Many of us justify our buying habits by saying we need cheap stuff to be able to provide for our families. While it's certainly good to provide a stable and healthy life for your kids, choosing an over-materialistic life — that couldn't exist without creating tragedy in the lives of the children in overseas factories who make products cheaply — cannot be the best way to accomplish that.

I'm not suggesting we become socialist or anything (this is a book about changing your world through capitalism, after all), and I don't think we're called to ditch our families (Jewish and Christian scriptures also have that whole "honor your parents" thing going on). But there is a line when caring for our children becomes spoiling them. That's not good for our own families, and it's certainly not good for our communities or for the poor who are part of those communities. Buying the bare essentials is kind of a no-brainer, but when it comes to extras like backpacks and video games and iPhones, maybe we should consider the opportunity to teach our children that the way we treat people matters (even if those people work in warehouses or in China where we can't see them), and that sometimes it's kinder to choose sacrifice than the latest technology.

Living in faith and saving money can coincide, but they aren't the same thing. In America, we treat earning and saving money as a sacrament, but it isn't one — not for pretty much any religion. Budgeting in and of itself isn't a problem, and it might be a great way of getting our spending back on a track in a way that honors God and our communities. But we can't confuse saving money with doing the work of God, because sometimes it isn't. Using the money we've been given wisely sometimes means saving, but often it means giving money to the poor, or spending a little bit more on our purchases to be sure we have vibrant communities and well-funded education budgets. It doesn't make sense to think God would want us to get things cheaper on the backs of the poor, which is what we're doing when we buy most things made in China, or when we shop at Wal-Mart. If God is calling us to save money, He's more likely calling us to go without — to sacrifice — rather than clip coupons and try to get more stuff for a cheaper price. Saving money can be healthy and responsible, but we've come to treat the savings account like a crutch or an idol. Building a stock portfolio isn't wrong, but it is wrong to do it at the expense of other human beings.

As religious people, we believe that God, not a 401K, is our only real hope for the future, and it follows that we should use our money in a way that's pleasing to him. On that list? Loving your neighbor. Taking care of the poor. Bringing glory to God. Making your money matter and not wasting what you have. Spending money in ways that lift up the people around you by showing love and respect. It's hard to place your life and your trust in a deity instead of a much more concrete-seeming savings account. But living in that murky place where you can't clearly see your future is what faith is all about.

WHAT WOULD JESUS BUY?

What we do with money is important no matter which religion we identify with, or even if we follow a different or more personal code of ethics instead of religion, but it's probably useful to take a close look at Christianity, the dominant religion in the U.S. Even if Christianity weren't the most popular religion in our country, it's the one that holds most control over our political system, and it certainly functions more than any other as an American business: Christians have their own massive book, music and clothing industries, and they make up a huge buying block with purchasing power that they're not afraid to throw around, whether it's spending money to back a cause they believe in (like they did for Chick-fil-A when they supported anti-homosexuality organizations), or withholding money by boycotting businesses that they don't agree with (like they did when JCPenney chose lesbian Ellen Degeneres as a spokesperson). For a religion that's supposedly based on servanthood, Christians are strangely unabashed power consumers. The meek may inherit the kingdom, but the rich are trying hard to establish squatter's rights.

The other reason my focus is Christianity is simply that I'm familiar with it. I grew up going to church almost constantly (three services a day wasn't unusual); I went to Christian schools my entire life (including college); my parents were Christian schoolteachers and Sunday School teachers, and my dad was a pastor. I've also read the Bible a handful of times and made a daily habit of individual study (including New Testament Greek). So while I'm certainly not qualified to represent the huge variety of Christian experience in America, it's fair to say I can give an informed insider's view of the evangelical tradition.

I've seen a lot of beautiful expressions of love and community in church, and I'm encouraged by the words and actions of clergy who stand up for our communities and for the poor (Pope Francis, in particular, provides a pro-servanthood, anti-materialism viewpoint that's encouraging). But I've also seen a lot of nastiness, a lot of politicians who use religion as vote-bait, and a lot of pastors who gloss over the greed of their congregations and of the church itself. Unfortunately, I think the latter is more representative of our reputation, and maybe of our legacy.

Jesus wasn't afraid to call the rich and powerful to account, but it seems that we are. The wealthiest members of our society identify as Christian. The same business owners who make the decisions to exploit child labor, who hire illegal workers, who keep wages low in order to make profits high, are in our churches every week. The rest of us are not immune, since we're propping up this system of abuse with our spending and with our investments. Where are the sermons addressing the impact of our obsessive consumerism? Which small groups are discussing the fact that our discounts come on the backs of the poor, and that our communities suffer when we prioritize sale prices over people?

As Christians, we claim to be children of the Creator, and we think that he designed us to be creative. I think that must mean that God cares about what we create — even what we create with our spending. When we see shopping only as consuming and acquiring, it feels like a one-dimensional experience, but in reality we are building something when we spend money. When we buy from a local shop, we put money into that shop and into the local economy. We create jobs. We put money into our city and state budgets, paving streets and building parks. We create better school systems, educating children both rich and poor and giving them the knowledge they need to grow up to create things we haven't yet dreamed of and to reach goals that we haven't yet been able to reach. We also create a sense of community, and we create freedom for individual expression and for individual choice over the quality and quantity of goods available to us. We create a healthier economy, more individual freedom, and a stronger community — and that is truly something beautiful. It's something worth our attention and our investment and certainly our sermons.

HASHTAG BLESSED

Our actions have consequences. Our purchases have consequences. What I learned during my year of small shopping is that those consequences don't have to be bad. When we give money to feed the hungry or to relieve poverty, we're living out the mission of Christ in a positive way. And when we refuse to give money to companies that perpetrate poverty, we're helping the poor in a different way.

Sometimes being the Good Samaritan means stopping to help the man on the side of the road. And sometimes it means not contributing to the system that pushed him down in the first place. Shopping locally was so good for me. It helped me pay attention to how I was spending money, and that helped me see myself more clearly. It kept me connected every day to the fact that I'm part of a community and that how I treat people matters. It was a profoundly spiritual practice in a way I never expected, and prioritizing kindness and thoughtfulness proved to be transformative. This is not about prose-lytizing and preaching; it's about caring for people. Yes, we still need to serve others in a hands-on way, but even with purchases that seem passive, we're helping to build up local prosperity, improving education and government services that help the poor and make the road out of poverty easier.

It's easy to minimize the suffering of minimum wage workers by saying, "It could be worse; they could be starving," while we drink our Starbucks in our SUVs. It's harder to look at people who are barely scraping by and admit, "It could be better for them, and I'm going to be sure my money pays into systems that make it better instead of funding oppressive corporations."

We should treat people with respect and support companies that do the same no matter our belief system, but even more if we worship a God who happens to demand it. Instead, we fund companies who create abysmal working conditions for foreign workers. We give money to corporations that treat American workers without respect and dignity. We demand discounts that mean laborers aren't compensated for backbreaking work. We buy from retail stores and food service chains that punish their employees for initiative and train them like machines instead of like people. As customers, we often don't act any better: We echo this treatment, yelling at our waiters and at the people behind the cash register.

This refusal to treat human beings as people is not a quirk of a few companies. It's an inherent flaw in the foundation of corporate America. In order to keep things cheap, you have to maximize sales and push your work force to churn out those sales at incredible speeds. Employees can't take pride in their work or individual creativity because it gums up the system. If we insist on cheap prices, we create the need for an automated work force where people are treated like machines and asked to work excessively long hours. It's not that difficult, physical work is necessarily inhumane; humans have always had to lift heavy loads, work long hours, and sacrifice our bodies for survival. But these laborers should be compensated, should have good work environments when possible, and should get breaks and health insurance. The big box system of free shipping and deep discounts simply means they do not.

In the United States, many of the wealthiest people, both the one-percenters and those of us in the middle class and its periphery, identify as religious and as Christian in particular. We also seem to be the first to suggest that poorer people could move up if they showed work ethic and initiative. When we talk and act this way, we're proving ourselves to be out of touch and arrogant. Even those of us who come close to being "self-made" have gotten our own handouts, advantages and help along the way, and our pretending that we didn't perpetuates a fiction that's dangerous to others and to ourselves. We forget about the times our parents bailed us out of tough financial situations. We forget that good education is its own kind of wealth, and that, even if we started with a firm foundation and zero money, we still had more than most people. Some of us forget that being white or being male or coming from a certain family still opens doors that are closed to others. We like to reminisce about our own crappy jobs, forgetting that we worked those back-breaking, low-wage jobs when we were still in our twenties and had the bodies and budgets to handle it — our situation just isn't comparable to that of minorities who grew up in underfunded school districts and without mentors, role models or supportive friends. We might've pulled ourselves up by our bootstraps, but somebody gave us the bootstraps.

Too often, we mix up Christianity with the Puritan work ethic, forgetting that Christ doesn't tell us to pull ourselves up by our bootstraps or become profiteers. There might be a lot of debate over what Jesus actually said, but it's clear that he didn't view fair working conditions or basic human decency as luxuries. He was pretty into loving one another and lifting up others who cannot lift themselves. I'm not supposed to sit comfortably in my own worldview and judge everybody else; putting my-self up on pedestal isn't encouraged, even if I did build the pedestal with my own two hands.

Unfortunately, judging other people is really easy and it feels awesome. If we tell ourselves that other people have less than we have because they *DESERVE* less than we have, because they didn't work as hard as we did, then we don't have to feel guilty or confused about life's unfairness. It's easier to accept being rich if we think it's because we earned it or because we are blessed: singled out by God for blessings. It's harder to face the truth that we are no better than our fellow human beings. That if we believe in a God, we also trust that what we have is a gift that we don't have the right to take credit for or to condemn others for not having. It would be interesting to see the results if we as Christians learned to act more charitably in our buying as well as our giving — and if our churches did the same.

SINNERS, SAINTS & CHEAPSKATES

Separation of church and state is pretty important. Maybe it keeps public prayer out of schools, but it also ensures that we can't be forced to participate in a religion we don't believe in, and it allows us the freedom to worship any way we choose. It's the reason we can go to church on Sunday and it's the reason we can choose to stay at home. It's a freedom that seems pretty basic to most of us in America, but only because we've never had to live without it. Our government doesn't have the right to control our religious institutions, which is pretty rad when you think about it. Not only are they prohibited from telling us what to say from the pulpit, but they can't even take our money; churches and other religious institutions don't have to pay taxes.

It's good that churches don't pay taxes because it protects us from government interference, but it doesn't absolve churches of the need to care for our communities financially. Since religious institutions benefit from streets, streetlights, emergency vehicles and other government services even though we don't pay for them, we have an even greater responsibility to buy locally — there's no need to take a free ride just because we can. We benefit from the system, so we should do what we can to pay it back.

In my experience as a shopkeeper, pastors and other people in charge of buying supplies for churches take the opposite view. They treat saving money like some kind of ministry, reasoning that the money they save buying discount can be better used to feed the hungry or help the poor. Theoretically, that makes sense, but spiritually and practically, the logic falls apart. For one thing, that money they imply goes to feed the poor could just as easily be going to putting on large-scale musical productions or paying the pastor a six-figure salary or cleaning the sanctuary. It could be going to paying for fancy printing on church bulletins or to buying matching team shirts for the choir trip or to producing a new worship CD. In fact, statistically, it's a lot more likely to be going to one of these things than to actually feeding the poor. The logic of helping the poor by "saving" money and buying from the very corporations who are keeping them poor just doesn't make sense.

If churches want to save money when buying supplies, they should do exactly what individuals can do — buy fewer things, but make them matter. The church exists to help our communities and show the love of Christ to others. Sometimes that means feeding homeless people and organizing clothing drives, and those are things churches tend to do well. But we should also pay attention to where we buy the food for those dinners and to who sells us the office supplies that help us organize for those events. We should buy locally for our books and Bibles, even when it's more expensive, because that's the kind of purchasing that helps people and helps our communities. Maybe it would be good for us to learn to do without, to sacrifice. Maybe that's part of what religion is all about.

Church leaders should remember that God doesn't calculate finances the way we do. This is a deity who says a woman who gives her last penny is giving more than the rich man who donates a sum that's technically higher, the God who says the oil in one jar can fill a dozen more, the dude who turned a couple of fish into a feast for thousands. When it comes to ministry, God doesn't seem to put much stock in physics or simple math; he's bigger and more mysterious than that. When Judas tried to stop Mary Magdalene from anointing Jesus, he reasoned that the money for the expensive oil could go to support the ministry and save the poor instead. That seems sensible, but scripture says that it wasn't. Budgeting for the ministry was the beginning of Judas's betrayal. We should be very careful before copy-catting his argument.

When Jesus kicked the moneychangers out of the temple, he was telling us that business, stockholders, profit-driven schemes and people who trust capital over God are not welcome in his church. The work of God is not saving money "for Jesus." The work of God is to be kind to people. To love people. To care for the poor. Jesus was pretty clear about this. He cared about individuals, skipping the "big impact" moves that would've reached millions, preferring to work one-on-one. Buying from small businesses helps as Jesus did, on an individual level. The money we spend at small shops helps the individual and it helps the community, putting money into schools and roads and government services that create a better standard of living for the poor. It helps your neighbors make a living, feed their children, and employ others. That makes it money worth spending.

THE PROFIT-DRIVEN LIFE

It's not just the church's outgoing money that needs a reformation; the way churches collect money, through tithing, is fundamentally flawed. It contributes to selfishness in the congregation, and it's part of the reason church members don't prioritize spending money mindfully or locally.

I've been pretty steeped in evangelical rhetoric for my entire life, but not everyone has (thankfully), so maybe you're not as over-familiar with a term like tithing as I am. In case you didn't go to Awanas (it's like scouts, but with Bible verses), here's a primer: Tithing is the practice of giving 10% of your income to the church. That's supposed to be the bare-minimum, baseline amount that you give, and you're encouraged to give an "offering" on top of that. No one forces you to give a tithe; they're not looking at your financials or asking for your bank account number (if they are, you're probably in a cult). But tithes are important, to pastors especially, because they're what keep the lights on at the church. They also pay the staff, keep the kitchen stocked with food for soup kitchens and potluck suppers, fill the baptismal with clean water, buy robes for the choir and support missionaries and mission trips around the world. The bigger the church, the more tithes it needs to make it run, so you can imagine the tithing needs of a megachurch that has a gym and amphitheater inside. Most pastors preach about tithing almost as much as they preach about the gospel (sometimes more), because their churches need money to stay open.

In order to keep the tithes flowing, churches some-times turn to prayer. They also turn to fund drives and slick marketing strategies designed to get people to open their wallets. Usually, these involve some passing of the offering plate, some market-driven messaging, and maybe an alter call. They definitely involve personal testimonies from people whose lives changed after they started tithing. This testimony is often given by a hus-band-and-wife team who stand together at the pulpit and talk about how their finances were in shambles until they took a leap of faith and started tithing. Miraculously, the money started pouring in. They bought a house, and maybe a new car. They sent their kids to college. God blessed them with a more comfortable life. I've seen couples claim that tithing allowed them to build a brand new house, and I've seen a woman claim that God bought her a BMW (I'm so not making this up). I've never once seen anyone acknowledge that tithing might not make you rich, and could actually make you poor, because sometimes we don't get what we want, even when we do what's right. God's math isn't one plus one equals two, and it's certainly not tithe plus time equals BMW.

This exploitation of tithing sets the tone for how we think about money from a biblical perspective, and when that tone is set to trying to get as much money as possible out of God, it's no wonder we don't think about shopping small. We don't think about what our spending could do for other people, because we're taught to be selfish with our money, even when we're giving it away. Promoting the fallacy that tithing leads to financial prosperity is not only false; it's also dangerous, because it encourages us to give not as a sacrament, but as an investment. That kind of reward-based giving isn't a sacrifice at all. Scripture rarely portrays comfort and wealth as a good thing, so the conclusion that material blessings are a reward for good behavior is somewhat dubious. Doing God's work because we're fishing for a particular blessing is setting ourselves up for disappointment (he tends to bless us his way, not ours). And expecting a financial handout in return for obedience makes a mess of our relationship both with money and with God.

LOVE IS NOT RUDE (BUT WE ARE)

In American churches, we're so obsessed with overseas mission work. I'm not saying we shouldn't be — taking the gospel all over the world is an important and beautiful thing. But it's also important to spread the love of Christ in our own cities and towns. Unfortunately, spreading the real gospel is harder than handing someone a tract or telling them Jesus loves them or writing a verse down on a receipt. As usual, Christ calls us to more. He calls us to actually engage people, and to meet them where they really are, focusing on respecting them and providing for their needs before we start with the verse quoting. Buying local is a great way to do that. It's a spiritual practice that helps us see our whole world differently. That's exciting, and it's also a huge responsibility.

I understand that interacting with people can be

a hard thing to do. I'm an introvert, and that means
sometimes I just want to go to a big box store so I can
ignore everybody. But as followers of Christ, we're called
to interact with each other. We're called to love each
other and not to pretend that the people we pass in
the aisles and the people we hand our credit cards to
are machines. People, even people working retail jobs,
deserve our interaction. Shopping small forces us to be
engaged. It forces us to interact. It makes us realize
that we're responsible for the impact we're having in our
communities and on other people, and that's exactly why
it's really difficult. Because that's not something we all
do naturally. It's not something we like to do. If it were,
Jesus wouldn't have had to work so hard to get us to
understand it.

Ask almost any retail worker or food service professional, and you'll get the same answer: Christians are the
worst. Christians are easily identifiable, partly because
we try to be: We wear clothes and jewelry and bumper
stickers announcing our religious beliefs, and every
Sunday morning we'll be the ones dressed up and cranky
while we wait in the Starbucks line. We're also easy to
spot because, well, we're mean. We tend to act self-ab-
sorbed and entitled. Maybe we really are worse than
other people, or maybe we're just more easily lumped
together because we dress alike — but either way, it's

a bad thing. Scripture says we should be known by our love, but we're mostly known for a tendency not to tip well, to leave a mess, and to treat our servers as sub-human just before we pray over our meals.

When we dress up on Sundays or proclaim our faith in other obvious ways, it's not enough to not be mean (although not being mean would be a good start). This is the time to be intentionally kind. Maybe we tip more, even if the service is bad. (Perhaps it wouldn't hurt us to practice mercy now and then.) Maybe this is the time to show compassion to the barista behind the counter instead of punishing them because you've had a long morning or the line was too long. This is the time to look your server in the eye, say thank you when it's appropriate, and limit your complaining. Keep a close eye on your children or keep them at home for lunch on Sundays if they can't behave. Tip generously. Bus your own table unless you're absolutely sure that's the server's job.

Christian misbehavior isn't limited to food service or to Sundays. As a barista at Starbucks and as a bookseller, my experience with other Christians has been overwhelmingly negative. I want to point out that a small number of Christians have been some of the most supportive and wonderful customers I've ever had. But the majority — to the tune of 95% — have been thoughtless and even cruel. They call me out for being single and childless in front of a line of people. They return their drinks more often, and they ask for discounts and coupons more often, and they want special treatment more often. Christians are the people who find books on the shelves of my store, buy them on Amazon, and then bring the books back into the store to read them, enjoying our free wifi and our comfy chairs without making a purchase. Christians are the ones who place bulk orders of devotional books but never pick them up or pay for them. Whenever we're tried to cater to Christians, we lose money, because they'd rather save a couple of dollars than support my job and the jobs of my coworkers.

Our Christian reputation for selfishness and stinginess is literally keeping people from the kingdom, and that's serious business. We can still go out to eat on Sundays. We can still have good service and good food. But if we want to act like self-important jerks, if we want to prioritize the number of dipping sauces we got with our chicken fingers over the soul of our server, we should at least go home and change into jeans before we go out. We should at least strip the Jesus fish stickers off our cars. The way to witness to a retail worker is not to invite them to church or to hand them a tract. It's to be kind. Behave the way Jesus would, and trust him to do the rest.

Obviously, we won't get everything right all of the time. Part of worshipping God is understanding that you are not him: We're human, and sometimes we'll end up treating people badly. We'll all buy from big box stores now and then, and that's okay. But just because we're not perfect doesn't mean we shouldn't try to represent our belief system in the best way we can. The poor will always be with us; we can't eliminate poverty. But we can adjust our purchases, our lives and our behaviors to remind us to remember them every day, in both big ways and small.

If I had known the world was ending, I would have brought better books.

—Dale Horrath
The Walking Dead

****

HEROES & VILLAINS:

Throwing Stones at a Giant

****

WE ONLY HAVE EYES FOR AMAZON

Amazon is my Voldemort. It's useless to pretend I can be impartial about everyone's favorite online retailer, because I can't. They're my soapbox, my nemesis, my own personal Goliath. But hating Amazon is like hating birthday cake: Everyone thinks you're crazy, and no one wants to even consider giving it up. (Who wants their birthday candles stuck into a meatloaf or a chicken pot pie?) Amazon has built up a tremendous amount of goodwill with their lightening-fast delivery, their free book giveaways, their rewards and their free shipping. Those smile-printed boxes arrive on our doorsteps almost as fast as we can order them, and for less than we'd ever dreamt we could pay for them. What's not to like?

I read a lot of books, and one thing they've taught me is that nothing comes free of consequences. When the White Witch offers you Turkish Delight, she's not being nice; she's manipulating you. When the Wizard makes promises he can't keep, it's time to pull back the curtain. Amazon is offering us the impossible: Exactly what we want as soon as we want it, and for less than it costs. Clearly, something's not adding up with this model. I don't think we're getting the whole story.

THE LOCALIST

The real story of Amazon, the one that includes blatant abuse of its workers, monopolization of markets, and centralized control of information, is mostly ignored by news organizations desperate for good-news stories and by bloggers who make money through Amazon advertisements. I hate to quote Rush Limbaugh about, well, anything, but the mainstream media has certainly failed us here. The media rarely cover corporate abuse. When they give us stories about local shops, it's usually when the indies are going out of business. Yet whenever Amazon changes the Kindle or Apple changes the iPhone, they get instant headlines. This isn't reporting the news as it happens; this is selective reporting and one-sided public relations spin. We're not getting the truth.

Instead of searching out stories, journalists cover product releases and corporate conferences, praising big business bullies and giving corporations free advertising without even attempting to cover both sides of the story. The Kindle gets plenty of headlines, but there wasn't a peep when Kobo made their internationally popular ereaders and ebooks available through America's independent bookstores. There's plenty of media coverage about the "dying" book industry, but none about the fact that the number of new independent bookstores has started to grow again.

This is lazy journalism, and it's a disservice to those

of us who depend on the news. When reporters are looking for innovators and entrepreneurial heroes, they should look local, but instead they usually cover the same old captains of industry — the ones that have already set our country off-course.

Even a supposedly unbiased (or liberal, depending on who you ask) station like NPR paints Amazon founder Jeff Bezos as a hero. They run stories on Amazon's entry into the grocery market without mentioning the impact on local farmers, stories about Amazon as a job creator with no coverage of the deplorable pay and working conditions at the warehouses they're opening (and no mention of the local businesses and jobs that will be lost when Amazon grows), and stories hinting that Bezos's purchase of *THE WASHINGTON POST* will save the newspaper industry like he "saved" books without talking about how dangerous his control of information could be. As one friend of mine put it, they're "trying to fill a Steve Jobs-shaped hole in the news cycle," but while Jobs was a pioneer and an inventor, Bezos is a profiteer. Making profits isn't necessarily bad, but it deserves a critical look from our news organizations.

It's true that Amazon is incredibly innovative: from the Kindle to drone delivery to content streaming, it's made some impressive advances in the way we shop, read, watch and listen. But as exciting as these innovations are, they're also scary, because they're happening in a competitive vacuum. Amazon uses predatory business strategies to bulldoze, not compete with, their rivals. They're poised to totally wipe out their competition sooner or later (probably sooner) This is a corporation that treats its employees like cattle, that tricks its way out of paying taxes, that considers choking customer freedom to be the cost of doing business. Amazon certainly isn't the only nasty corporation, but it is one that gets almost everything wrong. They don't support community; they don't treat people humanely; they punish their suppliers; they use their power to attack artists and innovators. They don't even use earth-friendly shipping methods.

Amazon is to online selling services what Wal-Mart is to other brick-and-mortar corporate stores: They're not the only one, but they're the biggest, and they're the worst. Amazon is even more dangerous than Wal-Mart, because they operate invisibly. They don't have big box stores and huge parking lots. They don't have light-up signs that shine into the night. We don't see them every day when we drive to work, so we have no idea how big they really are.

Of all the industries that Amazon attacks (and it's a lot of them), the book industry gets the most abuse. Control and manipulation of art and ideas is key to the success of Kindle and Amazon Prime. This isn't unique to Amazon; companies like Apple and Google are doing the same kind of thing. Amazon is more worrisome, not because no one else abuses the system, but because they abuse it so blatantly, and because they commit the greatest sins of big boxes with seemingly no shame or remorse. Amazon is on its way to having complete control of all books and all publishing, plus control of huge chunks entertainment-based streaming and journalism as well. When a corporation proves that it's willing to manipulate our access to information based on their bottom line, that's an attack on the spread of thoughts and ideas and stories. Whether we look at this from a market perspective, a philosophical one, or a historical one, that kind of control is, at the very least, troubling.

The sad irony is that books, the very product that's facing the most direct attack, warn us about what can happen in a situation where one entity has control over information. Amazon sells *BRAVE NEW WORLD*, *1984* and *FAHRENHEIT 451*, and they all warn about the effects of centralized control of power and information. Good science fiction is a manifestation not only of our greatest hopes and fears, but also of our possible future. It serves as a lens to help us see potential mistakes and avoid them, and it's sad that the world's biggest bookseller has become an instrument of informational control instead of the prophet that warns against it. We learn from Gollum in *THE LORD OF THE RINGS* that, when you're being controlled by the thing you love, it's time to let it go. It's easy to mock him for hanging on to his "Precious," but it's wise to remember that we might be in the dark as well, and our own idols aren't so easy to let go. The Amazon box bears a big smile, but no eyes. That seems, sadly, symbolic, because we're blind to its dangers and blissfully naïve of what problems the company's low prices can bring. Once Amazon controls the market, will they still prize cutting edge ideas and innovation? History tells us they won't, because they'll no longer have to.

Most news organizations close their eyes to Amazon's dangers in part because it's hard to report on Amazon. They're extremely secretive about their policies, and investigative reporting is expensive. Two media outlets that have covered Amazon are *THE NEW YORKER* and *Salon* (especially their excerpt from Simon Head's book *MINDLESS: WHY SMARTER MACHINES ARE MAKING DUMBER HUMANS*). These sources are thorough and respected (*THE NEW YORKER* in particular has notoriously detailed fact checkers), and the facts I use in this book are thanks to their reporting.

Why should we care about Amazon? Four main reasons:

They mistreat people

They don't pay taxes

Their monopoly is bad for competition

They control information and devalue art

THE COST OF DOING BUSINESS: GOODBYE HEALTH AND HAPPINESS

Internet-based companies tend to reject business-as-usual. At least in our imaginations, companies like Google and Twitter and Facebook are wonderful places to work. We hear about on-site gyms, organic cafeteria food, free childcare and bring-your-pet-to-work policies. We imagine exercise balls instead of chairs, beautiful glass buildings full of light, and an environment that encourages creativity. For a company like Google, our imaginations are probably close to reality. For a company like Amazon, this couldn't be farther from the truth.

Most of Amazon's employees work in warehouses, not in offices. That's not such a big deal; the problem is that each warehouse functions more like a prison than a workplace. Employees are immediately assumed to be thieves, and they're never treated any other way, regardless of performance. Workers are tagged with satellite chips that follow their every move. They're expected to walk miles of warehouse every day, carrying packages and sometimes getting on their hands and knees repeatedly without ever resting. If they're idle for as little as a couple of minutes, they can be reprimanded by text message, yelled at by supervisors and overseers, and presented with demerits. A worker in an Amazon factory is so micromanaged that, if he uses a bathroom other than the one located closest to his station, he must report the reason why to a supervisor, and if his reasoning isn't approved, he's punished like a naughty kindergartener.

Lunch breaks and quitting time don't provide relief either, because Amazon is so sure its employees are stealing that it forces them through required security checks that last from ten minutes to half an hour both times. This can cut a lunch break in half, and it means employees can't leave at the end of a long day. The kicker is that Amazon doesn't want to pay employees for this time. They require the long security checks for work, but they've argued to the Supreme Court that they shouldn't have to pay for them because the time isn't essential to job performance. To be clear, this means not only that Amazon is hoping to steal hours each week from their employees, but also that they're also trying to set a legal standard so we can all be abused by our employers and forced to work uncompensated time in order to keep our jobs.

Amazon relies heavily on temp agencies for labor not only so they can let people go without cause or without paying unemployment, but also so they can avoid paying health benefits to cover the physical trauma that comes from factory work. In a Pennsylvania factory where over-seers wouldn't allow air circulation from open doors even when the temperature shot past 100 degrees, employees were dropping from heat stroke so quickly that the town had ambulances lined up outside waiting for Amazon workers who had to be taken to the hospital. (The in-humanity of that is so disgusting that it's easy to forget the economic toll — thousands of dollars of emergency services and hospital bills that the government most likely assumed since Amazon avoids paying health care benefits.)

Physical abuse is bad enough, but this kind of treatment has psychological effects as well. Even at the corporate level, Amazon employees are reportedly never encouraged, routinely punished, and always asked for more. They cannot be innovative or creative. According to Simon Head, Amazon employs the creepy, Soviet-like slogan "one best way" to describe their policy of legislating the movements of their warehouse workers: It's not enough to pack a box efficiently; you must pack it in the "one best way," working your arms and body according to carefully scripted patterns of movement approved by the company. It's not enough to walk through the factory quickly; you must take the "one best way," turning where Amazon wants you to turn, walking at the speed they want you to walk, using the bathroom they want you to use.

Because Amazon is secretive about its policies, it's impossible for us to know exactly how far their abuse spreads. They do business in the cloud, and their warehouses are spread all over the world, so it's difficult to see their reach or the thousands of employees they impact daily. Because they operate in cyberspace, they don't have to pay taxes on the majority of their sales, meaning local economies — including employment rates — suffer. As Amazon customers, we're given everything we want, and we pay very little for it. But that doesn't mean it comes free: Amazon's employees pay dearly for our discounts and convenience — and so do our local economies.

BOOKSELLER, GROCER, INNOVATOR

Amazon's legacy isn't all bad. When it comes to creative problem-solving, the company actually does a lot of good. When most of the publishing industry had its head in the sand, Bezos's brainchild embraced books, using them to capitalize on the powerful new ordering and delivery capabilities of the Internet. They made book buying a fun, addictive process. Who knows if we're actually reading more books, but we certainly are buying them. Easy ordering, predictive search, and fast delivery means when we see that trademark Amazon smile on a box on the doorstep, we smile in return. Amazon is an innovator. They wrote an algorithm that recommends purchases based on what you've browsed and bought that's still a better predictor than any other online service in the book industry. They embraced ebooks early and have never let go, creating the Kindle, a device so popular that it's almost used as the generic term for ereader, regardless of brand.

Amazon positioned Kindle books so they're cheap and quick to download, and they realized that advances in technology and social media meant the self-publishing market was ready to explode in popularity. While most booksellers and publishers still blacklisted self-published authors (like me), Amazon embraced us, launching a self-publishing arm that took up where vanity presses left off and making book publishing a tangible dream for thousands of amateur and wannabe authors.

After having such great success in the world of books, Amazon has since expanded their reach, not only to other information sources (like Bezos's *WASHINGTON POST*), but to almost every consumer product under the sun. They stream TV, music and movies through Amazon Prime. They've experimented with selling paintings on the site and with delivering groceries. Now the company's even pioneering drone delivery, targeting USPS, FedEx and UPS (as they did with Barnes and Noble, Books A Million and Borders before Amazon rendered them largely irrelevant). Amazon pushes the envelope, and they've made books fun, easy and cheap. One ad for Amazon's streaming service shows a couple sitting on a couch, talking excitedly. "I don't know how they get it so cheap, but I'm glad they do," says the husband.

What that happy husband — and most of the rest of us — has forgotten is that, when something seems too good to be true, it often is. Amazon's spent quite a few years gathering power, and recently they've started to use it, bullying companies and customers who stand up to them. When Hachette, one of the biggest book publishers in the country, denied Amazon the increase in ebook profits that they asked for, Amazon struck back in a big way, making Hachette books difficult or impossible for customers to order. (Their tricks included taking ordering buttons off of Hachette titles, listing Hachette books as unavailable when they in fact had them sitting in their warehouses, and recommending that their customers buy "similar" cheaper books instead of the ones they wanted when they searched for Hachette titles.) Some people (most accurately — and hilariously — Hachette author Stephen Colbert) attacked Amazon for going after authors, but what's really distressing is that Amazon was willing to screw over its own customers, taking away our choice and our access to the books that we wanted to read. Their content decisions were based, not on quality, but on profit margins. Amazon excuses its warehouse abuses by claiming their customers, not their employees, are number one. But it's clear that the customer isn't the real priority, either — the bottom line is.

ALL OUR HEROES ARE VAMPIRES

It's fine for companies to protect their bottom line in a competitive environment, but when a corporation develops a monopoly, that greed starts to erode the market. We need more than just one company selling our products because capitalism needs competition to function well. Competition does pretty great things for our GDP, because when finding the best, most functional, most well-designed and rewarding products becomes necessary to compete, we become innovators again. This model rewards creativity; it rewards inventors who find new and better ways of doing things. It gives Americans incentives to put different and new products into our own economy and, by extension, the global economy as well. More diversity of products and more diversity of companies competing to make those products leads to more products and to better products, and it positions us at the cutting edge of invention once again.

Some people assume because I'm bookish and shy that I'm not into competition. When it comes to sports, they're right. This is partly because my dad's coaching advice — try harder; suck it up — didn't mesh with my sensitive teenage emotions, leading to a couple of very embarrassing public crying spells on the volleyball court. (And, uh, the softball field. And maybe once on a miniature golf course.) But for the people who think I'm not that competitive, I'm afraid the opposite is actually true: I'm so competitive that I won't even try something I don't stand a chance at winning. If you've seen me play volleyball, you know that I do not stand a chance at winning.

The sense of competition that plagued my partici-
pation in organized sports has served me better in the
rest of life. It's why I pushed to make excellent grades in
school. It helped me get the experience that I needed to
be a writer, to own a business, and to create this book.
Competition has its dark side, of course, but in my life
it's been useful in making me more creative and more
successful.

Our economy relies on this same principle. Businesses can compete against each other to make the
best choices and manufacture the best products, and
because they're driven to be better than each other, we'll
all theoretically end up with better products and a more
strong and diverse economy. The more businesses that
play a part in this competition, the better, because they
can all push each other. More voices also means more
variety and more development of niche products instead
of homogenized products that are okay for everyone but
not perfect for anyone.

More options are great for individual choice, and
they're good for our businesses too. Shopping small
means lots of different companies are involved in building our economy and creating products. Competition runs
wild, and the free market can do its thing. But when one
company controls a network of subsidiaries or franchises,

those stores generally aren't encouraged to compete with one another. New ideas get caught in red tape or get rejected because they don't fit into the accepted workflow of the business or into the broader goal of the parent company. Competition suffers, our country's economy suffers, and we as citizens suffer too. Lack of choice might make our decisions easy, but they ultimately make our lives and our communities weak.

If we choose a few big retailers instead of thousands of small ones, we'll be limited to the products that a few people are choosing. Start-ups without funding won't get the attention of these big box buyers, and their ideas and products won't ever make it into our shopping carts. Amazon's control of publishing and books is important not because I have a personal vendetta against the company, but because it provides a small-scale example of what could happen on a larger scale if Amazon continues to dominate more industries.

When books and publishing are run by big box stores and Amazon, a handful of book buyers decide which books to carry based primarily on trend-forecasting of which genres will be popular. They look at runaway successes in the industry and order more books on the same theme, giving no thought to whether or not the books actually tell good stories. Just look at the vampires — when *TWILIGHT* and *TRUE BLOOD* blew up, corporate stores filled their shelves with more stories of the undead, giving no thought to which books were actually good and which ones were sucking the lifeblood out of literature.

It's not that independent booksellers are good and big corporate stores are bad. It's just that independent booksellers speak independently of the corporate system, so by definition they represent lots of different viewpoints. Buyers from big corporations don't do that. Also, because hand-selling a book is a process that requires you to really stand behind the book (literally and metaphorically), local buyers prioritize good books — not necessarily intellectual and literary books, but books that are at least interesting, or have good characters, or tell great stories (ideally all of the above). It would be silly to say independent bookstores never sell bad books or order based on popular genre, but it would also be naïve to think they do it nearly as often. Independent retailers are incentivized to carry better books and to match customers with unique books because they can't rely on publisher kickbacks or bulk ordering rates to stay in business like big chains can.

Lack of choice and centralized decision-making isn't good for any industry. We don't want one buyer from Home Depot determining which hammer we can buy, one coffee buyer deciding whether we can have bold or medium roast, or one clothing retailer picking out sweaters for the whole country. This system isn't unique to books, but it's more important when it comes to books, because they aren't hammers or sweaters; books are ideas and stories and philosophy. They're the building blocks of society, and having a handful of people in charge of choosing which books we can read is a dangerous idea.

I like fun, trendy literature as much as the next Rob Pattinson-obsessed *TWILIGHT* fan, but cheesy books shouldn't be *ALL* we're offered. Less competition isn't good for our economy, and it's certainly not good for publishing. But when we buy from big box stores and from Amazon, we support that system, no matter which books we choose at checkout. If I buy from Amazon, I'm supporting the vampirization of literature, even if it's a Jonathan Franzen book that goes in my shopping cart.

YOU'LL BE LOYAL, AND YOU'LL LIKE IT

With Hachette, Amazon used their power to undercut a publishing company, but what will happen when someone writes a book critical of Amazon, and they decide not to sell it? (I guess we'll see, because I'm listing this book on Amazon to see if they'll sell it or censor it.) What happens when Amazon lets the government see their records so you can't freely buy a book without knowing you'll be on a government watch list? (Edward Snowden showed us that it's not paranoid to expect this kind of surveillance.) What happens if the next CEO of Amazon is anti-Semitic, or anti-Muslim, or simply chooses not to print the kind of books that you like to read? These aren't crazy questions. These are things that have happened too many times in history already. Instead of preventing them from happening, we're putting all the pieces in place to let them happen again, because we're giving control of the majority of book distribution to Amazon in exchange for free shipping. Once information is centralized, it's in a position to be controlled, and control of art and information has historically had a very poor effect on humanity.

Ebooks, while being a wonderful technology in many ways, make it even easier for a corporation to control your reading: Amazon doesn't have to burn your books, they just have to suspend your account, and all your books disappear in an instant. (This isn't theoretical; it has actually happened to Amazon customers.) Kindle is the most popular ereader in the U.S., partly because Amazon innovated and captured the market and our imaginations early. But part of Kindle's popularity comes from the fact that its devotees don't know how much their Kindles limit them, or that competitor ereaders like Nook and Kobo give their customers much more buying freedom and control over their libraries.

Kindle uses a specific ebook format that isn't compatible with anyone else's device, so it's impossible to buy your books from another store, and you can't read your Kindle books through another ereader, either. We don't actually own Kindle books. It's more accurate to say we're renting them, since those books are still under Amazon's control. They can, and do, shut users out of their libraries without notice; they've changed and removed books from Kindles without reader permission. They also prevent us from buying books from other sources, or from leaving Amazon and keeping the books we've paid for.

Big box stores have always used loyalty programs like discount plans and store credit cards to discourage us from buying from their competitors, but now that music, movies and books are traded digitally, they've stepped it up a notch, selling us art that is hard to enjoy on another device. Lots of companies, including Apple and Google, also make transferring digital content more difficult than it has to be. The difference is that those companies make it annoying to choose or transfer content from other companies, but

Amazon makes it impossible. What's best for the customer is sacrificed for what's good for Amazon.

BOOKS ARE CHEAP, AND THAT'S A BAD THING

Amazon paints itself as the Robin Hood of books. The company's mythology has it swooping in on a white horse, robbing Big Publishing of its selfishly hoarded riches and then riding through town, passing out books to the peasantry in the streets, putting stories directly into the hands of the people. But, like much of what Amazon sells, that's just fiction. Corporations aren't in the business of giving freely without hope of reward. So what's Amazon getting out of making books cheap — so cheap that they actually lose money on some of their books and Kindles?

Amazon's prices are low so they can put their competitors out of business, and so they can get us hooked on discounts and free shipping so we don't buy elsewhere. Lack of competition is ultimately bad for consumers, but having other book retailers knocked out is in the best interest of Amazon. It's not just booksellers they're going after: Amazon's book business functions as bait, luring customers in with cheap (sometimes below cost) books so we'll buy other products, download music and stream online content. In other words, they undervalue literature so we'll buy cell phones and Blu-ray players and subscription video service from them, all while pretending to promote reading. That tactic has a lot more in common with the business model of the corner drug dealer than it does with Robin Hood.

When Amazon sells a book cheaply, it's cutting out dozens of jobs — several of which would be in local communities — along the way. When they slash the price of a book in half, they're making sure neither authors nor local booksellers (or the communities where they have jobs) can profit from book sales. Even without Amazon's price cuts, nobody's raking in cash from books (the only person getting rich through publishing these days is J.K. Rowling, and she has magic on her side); authors and booksellers don't need to get wealthy, but they do deserve fair wages for their work. A book should cost money because it costs money to produce, but more than that, because it has an artistic value that we should protect.

Accepting a purely profit-based standard for industries like books that are essential to our humanity is particularly devastating to people who live in poverty: The cheapest food is the most unhealthy food, and the cheapest art, free entertainment, is often vapid, over-sexualized and incredibly violent. Community art is too rarely supported either on the street or in school, and, if companies like Amazon have their way, books will soon be unavailable to anyone who can't afford an ereader. Because we're not funding our community tax systems through local shopping, the education system in low-income communities no longer includes music and theater programs, and even getting access to libraries and stories has become difficult.

Poorer people are missing out on access to art and ideas, to books and music, and even to food that isn't slowly killing them, because corporations don't have the poor in mind when they make decisions. When all of our decisions are driven first and foremost by profits, the poor are cut out of the equation. So are any ideas and any art that don't clearly make money or lead to profits. It's not the job of the government or of corporations to subsidize art, but it is wrong for them to make art and ideas inaccessible to our citizens, or for one company to take control over so much information. That doesn't make a productive society — not for those who live in poverty, and not for the rest of us, either.

Amazon's use of books as a strategy to draw people to other parts of your business doesn't exactly show a commitment to art and literature. This Robin Hood is robbing the poor of their voice and their access to ideas. That's not altruism; that's highway robbery. Selling books for less than they cost and less than they're worth doesn't get more people reading. It might get more people to drop books into their virtual shopping carts like packs of gum at the cash register at Target, but it certainly doesn't encourage them to value, or even read, the books themselves. It's also forcing a monopoly instead of allowing competition to thrive and strengthen our economy.

BOOKS, MAGIC AND GARAGE ENTREPRENEURS

Our nation was founded on words, on printed pamphlets that questioned the powerful, and on a Constitution that gave a voice to the powerless. It sounds melodramatic to say our society will crumble when our books disappear (partly because that's the plot of many sci-fi novels), but it's also what's actually happened, not just in fiction, but in history. Nazis controlled books. Fascists controlled books. Communists controlled books. Those movements were also largely started by books, so their founders knew their power and fought to control and limit other voices. That same control is being put in place right now, this time by businesses instead of a government. Corporations now control not just which books are sold, but which books are published, and by extension, which ideas make it into the hands of the people. That kind of control is bad for our hearts and minds and freedoms — and it's bad for competition and our economy, too.

Books are important to me for so many reasons. I like reading them, reviewing them, and (now) even writing them. When I was younger, books were my escape, my comfort, and the place I went to dream. As an adult, they still do those things, but they're also the way I learn about people who think differently than I do and who live lives that look nothing like mine. They've made me more empathic and more able to be present in the lives of my friends, family, and even strangers. And they've been my continuing education, the way I learned how to eat more healthfully, to build a freelance career and to build a brick-and-mortar business. Books have made me a better writer, a better friend and a better person. When I don't know how to do something, I read about it, and as my knowledge grows, so does my perspective: I've become less judgmental, less arrogant, and more willing to compromise and admit when I get things wrong (which happens pretty often — see, I've admitted it). I don't want to imagine my life without books.

It's not overstating the point to say we haven't seen

a change in the way we process reading as dramatic as the Internet and the ereader since Gutenberg. As a history nerd I'm incredibly excited to be alive at a time of such an amazing invention and change in the way we read: Information can spread rapidly and not necessarily be limited by income level or location, and books can legitimately get cheaper once they're freed from the restrictions of print. The book industry went through our digital metamorphosis so long after music and film went through theirs (the Kindle launched almost a decade after Napster did) that I felt sure publishing, an industry based on reading and learning, would avoid the mistakes made by those who went before us.

I was wrong. Publishers made the same mistakes big music labels made, trying to control artists and content and charging way too much for digital versions. And big publishing refuses to work together to create a functional digital system: Bafflingly, printed books don't even come with free digital downloads like vinyl records and many movies do, and some ereaders (well, the Kindle) can't even handle books from other publishers. Instead of learning from the stories of the film and music industries, book publishers are remaking the same mistakes. Publishing houses were already fighting each other and fighting progress before Amazon came along to exploit their weakness and outperform them all.

As a publishing friend of mine put it, "The book industry is like a kid on the playground getting beat up by the bully that is Amazon. You want to yell, 'Fight back! Just try to fight back!' But they just stand there getting punched." I was tired of seeing books get sucker-punched, so I did the only thing I knew to do: In the age of diminished profits, when ebooks threatened paper and Amazon threatened everyone, I opened a bookstore.

*I want to work!
I want to build
something of my
own; how do you not
understand that?*

— Don Draper
Mad Men

****

DIARY OF A SHOPKEEPER:

My Life in the
Trenches as the Owner
of an Independent

****

SO LONG, STARBUCKS

You don't hear a lot of stories about an independent shop taking over a Starbucks. It always seems to go the other way around — the big bad wolf of a corporate store takes over the mom-and-pop. But in this little-business-that-could story, it's the big box that bit the dust and an independent shop, Church Street Coffee & Books, that took its place in the same building that used to be a Starbucks. You can still see a few clues around the shop of our heritage: We've left the tables in the same places, those 90s-style swirly mirrors are still in the bathrooms (we tried everything we could do to get them off the wall, but they wouldn't budge), and we even salvaged our trash cans and counter mats from the dumpster where Starbucks left them behind. They gave us our sound system, our countertops, and our walk-in refrigerator — but they gave us something a lot more important than that, too.

Starbucks gave us a story to build on when we created Church Street. I'd worked there, and so had my business partner, Cal. He'd been my manager at Starbucks, and he was a personality tour de force. He danced behind the counter, celebrated Talk Like a Pirate Day, ran a Bible study group comprised mostly of baristas from our store, quoted Chris Rock ad nauseam, smoked like a chimney and always had time for deep philosophical questions, even in the middle of the morning rush. He taught us to always prioritize customer connection over filling in our Coffee Passports (yes, that's a real thing), and we were referred to as "black sheep" and "Cal's Motley Crew" in emails from management. One of our baristas called our store, Starbucks Crestline, "the mom-and-pop Starbucks that never was." That turned out to be truer than any of us expected.

I can honestly say that I never once thought about turning our Starbucks into an independent while I still worked there. Even when Cal called and asked me if I wanted to open a shop with him, telling me he'd heard a rumor that Starbucks Crestline was closing, I didn't believe him. His premonition was mostly based on speculation, and I couldn't imagine that Starbucks would shut down a moneymaking store, even if the profits weren't as high as they once were.

When he called me with the idea, I was actually at our Starbucks, sitting at my favorite table (the one by the huge picture window that's close enough to the espresso machine that I can talk to baristas). Cal was excited — really, really excited. He wanted to start an independent coffee shop, and he wanted to make it a bookshop, too. He asked me if I thought it would work and if I'd come on as a partner — because we worked together well and because I knew the book business. I told Cal I was interested, but not because I actually believed it would work out. He just seemed so excited and full of hope that I didn't want to be the one who crushed his dreams.

I'd always thought about owning a bookstore or a café in sort of a vague way, and this was clearly an unbeatable opportunity. The space was already built out as a coffee shop, so our renovations would be doable. Cal and I worked together well and really knew our businesses, so I knew we could manage the shop well. But most import-ant, we already knew our community. Combined, we'd worked in the area, Mountain Brook, for about 15 years, and we both enjoyed our customers and had a good idea of what they were looking for in a shop. We already had relationships, and I felt sure we could build on them to create a successful business. It was pretty clear that, if I ever wanted to own my own shop, my ship had come in — it was time to get on board or admit that I never would.

When I got home the first day that Cal and I talked, the first thing I did was throw up; that's how stressed out the idea of the store made me, and how scared I was about taking a chance on a new business. I tried to forget about the bookstore (I don't usually take vomit-ing over an idea as a good omen). But it soon became clear that it wasn't going away: Starbucks did close, Cal and I found investors, I quit my job, and we opened our shop, Church Street Coffee & Books — all within six months after that initial call. In case you're not familiar with small businesses, six months is an incredibly short amount of time to open a business in. Like, "you're insane" short. Like, "in six more months, you'll be out of business" short. When I started Shop Small and gave up big box shopping, I was prepared to give up on Starbucks. But that little shop in Crestline wasn't going to give up on me so easily.

WRITING THE CHURCH STREET STORY: THE MOTLEY CREW TAKES OVER

Stories are important because they help us understand and navigate life. Cal and I are both hugely addicted to books and story, and that shows in the way we built our business. Even from the beginning, we did what we could to bring together the cast of characters who'd already played important roles in our lives for years. It was the Judd Apatow style of hiring, I guess — bring in who you've worked with before and leverage the camaraderie and chemistry that you've already built into a new work of art. It's a cliché to say the shop was built with love, but in our case it really was created by people we loved and who loved us back, and specifically with people we'd worked with in our other shops.

My former bookselling coworkers from Jonathan Benton are the first people to be there for me when I need them to come in for a book club or an author event. When we got our first massive delivery of books, it was these friends who came to help me organize inventory, alphabetize and shelve a huge number of books. We sat on the floor eating Mexican food and drinking beer while they let me boss them around for hours, and they did it all for free. One of my favorite memories of opening day at Church Street is looking over at the window seat and seeing this group sitting together and drinking coffee.

The baristas of Starbucks have come through for us over and over again, too. They were some of our first customers, and some of the first people in line to help with the business: Daniel did amazing work on our menu boards. Emily joined us as a barista and baker. Robby and Gregory pinch-hit for us when we needed help behind the bar. Heath developed our tea selection through his work at Two Leaves and a Bud. And there are two former Starbucks baristas in particular, Sri and Courtenay, who both have put hundreds of hours of work into the store and helped shape it into the community that it is today.

Sri's a bit of a legend in certain Starbucks circles. He'd worked with Cal years before, and since then he'd risen to a high rank at Starbucks. He's fantastic at quality control and training (I'd had him as a teacher for a few management trainings while I was still at Starbucks), but Sri's real magic isn't in his resume, impressive though it is. He's just a great human being. He's kind and hilarious (we call it "Srilarious") and weird and wonderful. As a barista, he's a little bit psychic, somehow knowing just what each customer wants before they order it (or at least convincing them it's what they wanted after he's already made it). Everybody loved Sri, but at the time, Sri was very rooted at Starbucks. So when Cal called and said he thought he could convince Sri to come work for us and asked what I thought we should give him to entice him to come, my answer was simple: "Give him whatever he wants." Sri's been with us since the day we opened.

Bringing my sister, Courtenay, on board was huge because she designed the interior our store. She's the reason you don't have to reach over people drinking their coffee in order to grab a book off the shelf, and she's the reason we have a reading nook and a kid's section in what used to be a closet and an unused hallway. She worked for Cal even before I did as a barista at Starbucks, so she understood what coffee customers were looking for, what baristas needed to do our jobs, and where to put the condiment bar. She also worked within our budget (which was embarrassingly low), and she kept me from turning the entire shop into an homage to Harry Potter and Cal from turning it into a hippie-style art gallery. My parents put dozens of hours of work into helping with our build-out and painting the shop, and it was wonderful to see them come alive as they helped me build my business and helped make my sister's vision a reality at the same time.

The last big piece was Heather, Cal's wife. Heather was a ballerina by trade, and she'd been a stay-at-home mom raising her and Cal's wild bunch: Bain was five when we opened the store, Coulter was three, and Mattie was one. Heather happened to be an extraordinarily talented home cook. She has skills, and even more rare, she has the ability to make food that has a comforting and rich flavor. Real ingredients are important to her, and she's a lot more interested in making sure everything tastes amazing and everyone really loves what they're eating than in making anything trendy or fancy. Heather developed our menu by gathering favorite recipes she'd compiled through the years and adjusting them to taste even better.

Unlike a corporate store, we couldn't treat our staff like numbers even if we'd wanted to. Our staff is like family to us — in the case of Courtenay and Heather, they are literally our family. I won't pretend we have close-knit relationships with every barista who walks through our doors, but we do care about them all on a personal level. We've had to discipline people and even fire people, but unlike at corporations, we do that only when there's no other option. There's simply no wall separating us from our employees, so we see them as people instead of a collection of write-ups and reports.

THEY LIKE US. THEY REALLY LIKE US!

We didn't have a lot of advantages (i.e., we didn't have a lot of money), but Cal and I did have one major asset over a lot of the dreamers who open their own stores: I'd already managed a bookstore, and Cal had already run a coffee shop, and both of our previous stores were in the same neighborhood where we eventually set up shop. That was super important, both because we made our mistakes with other people's companies (sorry, Starbucks), and because we knew our customers before we opened our doors. The ability to make decisions based on what our customers wanted saved us from a lot of fights and a lot of mistakes. It also paid off, because people really love Church Street.

We thought they'd love our locally roasted coffee, but they didn't. (Well, not at first — the switch from Starbucks' darkest-of-the-dark roast to our you'll-love-me-once-you-get-to-know-me lighter roast was a tough transition for some of our regulars.) But even from the beginning, we had great feedback on our book selection. I'd put it together, so obviously I'd hoped people would like it, but the fact that they embraced our concept so quickly and so eagerly was a complete surprise. See, we don't have a full bookstore with wall-to-wall shelving. We have a small number of titles, but each one has been vetted in some way: Either we've read it, or it's been recommended by someone we trust. I thought people would be confused about why we weren't set up traditionally, but they seemed to get it right away.

Most people say they love that they can come in and pick up any book and know that it will be good. They like not feeling overwhelmed by choices. They like being able to let their kids pick out any book in the store and say yes, not having to wonder if it's trashy or badly written. Our books were a hit. Our drink sales were strong. And it took us a little while to figure out how to run a bakery, but once we did, our pastries really hit their stride, and we now have one of the most popular cookies in town.

Cal and I managed our stores very differently, but our styles turned out to be just as complimentary as we'd hoped. He blasted Michael Jackson on the morning shift, danced for customers, and asked about everybody's kids by name. I played The National and Sun Kil Moon in the afternoon, recommended books, and commiserated with customers hoping to salvage their long workdays with cookies and mochas. Cal streamlined our brewed coffee system so we'd come closer to the tastes of the morning customers while still getting them in and out in time for work, and I brought in the Yerba Mate Latte, soon to be one of our more popular signature drinks. I'm good at planning to prevent as much chaos as possible, and Cal's better at dealing with the chaos when it comes (and it inevitably comes when you own a small business, especially a food-based business).

Our customers also embraced our staff. Whenever our shop is reviewed or profiled, the writer mentions the friendliness of our baristas, and that's not an accident. We try to teach our baristas that it's important to be kind to people, and our customers respond to that — not just by buying more, but by returning that kindness to us as well. (Well ... for the most part.) Cal and I had dreamed of creating a store that was a real community center, that felt welcoming to whoever walked in the door. Church Street became that kind of shop earlier than we'd ever imagined, and I'm incredibly thankful to our friends, our staff and our customers for making that happen.

Ours is the kind of shop that feels like it's always been there, that seems to organically belong in the neighborhood. In most ways, that's very good. But it also means that a lot of people will never recognize how it got that way. Church Street is what it is because Cal and I worked really hard to make it that way. But it feels so natural, so organic, that the majority of people think we just stumbled into it, and they don't realize the strategy that went in to creating the business. Usually, that's just fine. On my bad days, I wish more people understood that we're successful partly because we're good businesspeople, not losers who got lucky. But then I remind myself that I went into business to have a shop, not to get praise. And anyway, even the smartest entrepreneurs need more than good strategy to be successful, and we've certainly had a lot of luck along the way, too.

WE'VE GOT FRIENDS IN SMALL PLACES

I knew the statistics about local shops giving back to their communities before we started Church Street — that, from every $10, anywhere from $1 to $6 more recirculates into local communities from purchases made at local shops. And I knew why, theoretically: because small shops tend to buy from other local shops, and because they give more to charity. But it wasn't until we opened the shop that I really understood why or how that happens.

Purchasing for a store on the wholesale level is pretty much the Bizarro World version of purchasing as an individual consumer. Technically, the logistics are pretty much the same, but the experience, everything from order fulfillment to customer service, is completely opposite. When I order something for myself, I can usually trust that I'll get exactly what I ordered, that it will come on time, and that my service experience will be good and reliable. Ordering for the shop is a very different, and usually very frustrating, experience.

Customer service at the wholesale level is inconsistent at best, and it's shocking how many of shipments arrive incorrect or incomplete. Orders are marked fulfilled weeks before they're actually sent out. We've been shipped lids that didn't fit their cups. We've been shipped a box half-full of sugar packets that were completely emptied of their sugar. We've been shipped entire orders of books that were supposed to go to other bookstores while ours went missing. It's not an exaggeration to say 30% of our orders are under-stocked or just plain wrong, and we're not just unlucky — this is pretty much the industry standard. So when the statistics say that local shops are more likely to buy local, it's at least partly because it's much easier to get a guy to drive across town and fix your order than it is to get him to drive across the country, and orders have to be fixed so often that this kind of turn-around is important.

At Church Street, most of our stock, from our cups to the coffee we pour into them, comes from local suppliers. We buy indie partly because we like to shop small, but mostly because buying local is actually the practical solution. If we underestimate the demand for Peppermint Mochas, we can make a run for more peppermint syrup immediately. If someone accidentally drops a whole sleeve of cup lids on the floor, more are delivered after one phone call. And if we get the wrong order of, say, coffee, we can have replacement beans within an hour.

Wholesale ordering is always sketchy, even at the corporate level. That's why most big box stores have their own fulfillment centers. They don't buy local because they have the buying power to own both the wholesale operation and the storefront. This is good for the corporation because they don't have to deal with the pitfalls of mass ordering or of ordering from hundreds of different local distributors (at least not at the store level), but it's bad for the community where the storefront operates, because it means that much more money is being funneled out of the local area.

Local stores create a lot more tax revenue, but we give more to charity, too. At Church Street, this proves true: We give — a lot. Every day (usually more than once), we're asked to donate money, or buy sponsorship advertising, or give coffee or books to an organization's auction. We usually try to do it, especially if the person asking is a regular customer (although it's astonishing how often people who never buy from our store ask us for favors, and how offended they get when we say no).

This is partly because we're soft-hearted pushovers, and it's partly because what's good for our community is good for us. Donations are also a good way for us to advertise, because charity donations are usually credited to the organization, and it's a tax write-off. Besides all that, we say yes pretty often because it's really difficult to look someone in the face and say no. A request for corporate giving gets stuck in red tape, and the person denying your request never has to look in your eyes and tell you that your organization doesn't deserve their money. I do, and it's part of the reason I'm more likely to say yes. Even if your local shop doesn't have a touchy-feely sucker like me at the helm, they're still likely to give to charity because of the tax incentives, because it's cheap marketing, and because they want to avoid the bad word-of-mouth you're likely to give them if they turn you down.

At Church Street, we buy local and give local because it makes sense for our business, but we also do it because we know that a strong community of local businesses makes our own shop stronger. We're lucky to have neighbors who agree, and our fellow independent business owners and managers were amazing when we started Church Street. They welcomed questions about their business practices and their suppliers. They commiserated when the business got so tough it seemed like it would break us. They sent their customers over to us for coffee and cookies. It was like we were all in the same fraternity, and we got there by being hazed by our own businesses. Our local shop owners and staff were an incredible bright spot on the sometimes-bleak horizon of opening a business, and I'm so thankful for that. I'm proud to know them; I'm proud to do business with them. And I try to pay it forward, giving advice and help to new businesses and start-ups who ask me for it.

But even if we didn't like our fellow business owners, Church Street would probably buy from them anyway. It's important to know that local shops don't support each other because we're good people, or because we think other shop owners are nice. We do it because it makes good business sense for a small business to buy from other local businesses. Corporations don't buy local because it doesn't make sense for their businesses to do it. This is an important distinction, because it means that the inherent structure of a locally owned store is geared toward putting money back into the community, while the corporate structure is set up to send it away. No matter who's running those businesses, this financial breakdown is likely to hold true. This is true at Church Street, and statistics show that it's true on the Main Streets of the rest of the country, too.

LITTLE SHOP, BIG EXPECTATIONS

Partly because Church Street is located in an old Starbucks, we work very hard to maintain the level of service our customers were used to before we switched from corporation to independent. We prioritize the Starbucks standard of "speed of service," trying to get drinks served quickly so busy people can keep moving. We have a big menu with a huge variety of drinks meant to satisfy every palate. We're open every day until 10 p.m. to compete with chain coffee stores and their long hours. But it's not enough to keep up with Starbucks; we're expected to be better than they are, to offer all that they do plus the flawless customer service and attention to detail that you'd hope for in an independent.

As consumers, we hold independents to a higher, and maybe impossible, standard that we don't require of big box stores. I know, because I do the same thing. If a shelf is empty at Target, I assume the product was an exceptionally good seller and that they'll have more soon. But when I can't find what I'm looking for at a small shop, I think, "Stupid independents never have what I want." When someone's rude to me at Starbucks or Whole Foods (that's a little joke — no one's ever rude at Whole Foods), I shrug it off. But when I get the same attitude at an independent, I think, "Well, *THIS* is why no one ever shops here," and I don't go back. I don't know why we do this, but I think it's partly because it feels fruitless to get angry at a big box store because there isn't anyone to direct the anger at. Who're you going to call to complain to? Mr. Wal-Mart?

When people come to Church Street, they know they can complain to me, and lots of people like to take advantage of this small shop perk. People say things to me that they wouldn't dream of saying at a Barnes and Noble or a Starbucks. I've been yelled at in a crowded café. I've had a gift card thrown in my face by an angry customer. More than one self-published author has shouted at me out of anger that I wouldn't carry their books, and several male customers have asked to speak to "the man in charge" when I didn't let them have their way. Once, a customer accidentally dropped her fork and then complained to me that our plates were too slippery.

Coffee is a business based on ritual. You like to have your "usual." You like to add a packet of sugar, and pour in a touch of cream, and stir it all up just so. Part of the reason Church Street has such a loyal customer base is that you wake up literally craving our products. Caffeine and sugar are addictive, but it's not just your brain that likes the coffee shop; you probably want it emotionally, too. (Okay, emotions are also controlled by the brain — shut up, science nerds.)

Complaining — sometimes about the exact same things every time — is just another part of the coffee ritual for some people. At Starbucks, we had one customer who came in every single night to ask for a Venti decaf coffee at 9 p.m., and every single night she'd act surprised that we didn't have any made. (For anyone wondering why coffee shops don't brew decaf at night, it's because we can't sell it. Apparently, most people who want decaf are already at home, watching TV or settling in with a good book and tucking themselves into bed by nine at night.) Anyway, she kept coming into Starbucks, and she kept acting surprised, night after night. When we opened Church Street, Venti Decaf came to see us, too — once or twice. She ordered decaf, and she got the same response (if anything, I was nicer to her than I'd ever been at Starbucks). After that, she stopped coming at all. She was willing to keep trying Starbucks for five years, but she gave up on us after a week.

I wish all of us — including the Venti Decaf Lady and myself — would consider giving local stores a little more slack. We're doing more work than the big guys, and we have less to work with in the first place. We have to be good at everything and masters at some things. We're dealing with the stress of balancing the books, the drama of managing a staff, and the irritating realization that yet another light bulb has to be replaced. (Why are there so many different kinds of light bulbs in our store? It's infuriating!) We have to be good at fixing toilets and planting perennials in our outside flowerpots and convincing the zoning board to grandfather in our signage, and that's what's going through our minds while we're chatting with you and making your cappuccino. The balance of power between locally owned stores and corporations is dangerously out of whack. As consumers, one way we can change that is to adjust our expectations, requiring more from corporations and cutting independents a little slack.

BIG BUSINESS BULLIES

We're certainly not getting any slack from corporations. Big companies spend so much money lobbying because having the law on their side works to their advantage in the long run. Sometimes this means tax breaks that favor big business. Sometimes it means strict copyright and patent laws that make it easier for corporations to shut out their competition.

Big box stores "steal" from independents all the time — look at Amazon's push to reward its customers for going into brick-and-mortar stores and taking cellphone pictures of products and prices — but they're the first to sic an army of lawyers on an independent that crosses into their territory. At Church Street, we go out of our way not to copy drink recipes or name a drink anything that could be the property of Starbucks. If we aren't careful, a seemingly innocent drink covered in whipped cream and caramel drizzle could become the target of a lawsuit.

In the summer, blended coffee is big business. At

Starbucks, we had such a huge after-school crowd that I'd literally just yell out the Frappuccino names and have the kids raise their hands for the ones they wanted so I could make them in big batches. "Who wants Vanilla Bean! Who wants Strawberries and Cream! Who wants Chocolaty Chip!!!" I'd yell — I had to yell, because these were middle school kids, and if middle school kids are two things, they are smelly, and they are loud. Oh, and they are messy. And ... never mind. Anyway, I've used a blender enough to last a lifetime, and I've come home smelling like rancid whipped cream more times than I'd like to admit (yeah, it's as disgusting as it sounds). Starbucks actually had to have their grease trap cleaned out about every six months, and it was just from whipped cream. That's how much whipped cream was *GOING DOWN THE DRAIN* — enough to clog up the back sinks and make the whole prep room smell like there was a dead body in the dish sanitizer. I don't want to think about how much whipped cream went into the customers.

The point is, people like their Frappuccino. So when we started Church Street, we created a blended iced drink of our own. We didn't steal the recipe, because we opened the store with 90% ex-Starbucks baristas, and if there's one thing to know about Starbucks baristas, it's that we freaking hate Frappuccinos (the story above is just the tip of the iceberg). Cal and Sri created an original recipe that's pretty much as far away from a Frappuccino as you can get while still containing milk, sugar, espresso and ice (which actually isn't that far away, really). We called it the Church Street Frost.

When we describe Frosts to customers, they say, "Why don't you just call it a Frappuccino?" We don't call it that because we would get sued, and sued hard. Starbucks is pretty famous for keeping an eagle eye out for copyright infringement. This is the company that copyrighted "venti," the Italian word for "twenty," so you really don't want to mess with them when it comes to naming. Lots of independents have stepped on Starbucks' toes, and they come down pretty hard. That's fair, but what's not fair is that big businesses can steal ideas from local shops all they want with no recourse, because independents don't have the resources to protect their intellectual property, recipes and naming ideas.

The problem is not that Starbucks is allowed to protect its silly drink names. The problem is we've stopped protecting all businesses in favor of protecting only big businesses. Our laws favor corporations, and so the market favors corporations, but this isn't a free market at work — this is a market that's skewed toward protecting the companies that are already the biggest and the strongest. Government and lawmakers are clearly on the side of big business, and the parties that claim to be all about the free market — the Republican Party and the Tea Party — are, ironically, the worst offenders. We've started protecting Goliaths and taking the slingshots away from the Davids at the same time.

The law is slanted far in favor of huge corporations. Even the money that is earmarked for small businesses often goes to corporations in the form of their franchises: Companies like McDonald's and Chick-fil-A get government support that should be going to real entrepreneurs but is instead used by the local owner of the national chain. This is bad because the lion's share of the income from franchises still goes to the parent corporation, not the local owner. And it's bad because it doesn't allow for diversity of offerings or strategy, which, as we know, cripples American innovation. These big box businesses get tax breaks. They're bailed out if they fail. They get government contracts. And they have a leash on Congress because of their money and their lobbyists, so they're effectively sponsoring government policies.

Before I started a business, I assumed that start-ups get a lot of governmental support. Promoting entrepreneurship and local business is one of the few talking points that both Democrats and Republicans put in their speeches. It's one of the only issues that has bi-partisan backing, so I assumed Congress had small business's back. Starting my own business was a harsh wakeup call about the difference between talking points and political action.

In fact, Congress has corporate lobbyists in their ear, and most of that "small business" talk is only talk. When politicians speak about small business, they aren't talking about businesses like mine, seriously tiny shops on America's Main Streets. They're talking about businesses that employ hundreds of people, that are slightly smaller than big corporations. These businesses are important, too, and it's better to support them than the seriously huge businesses, but it doesn't address the real issue of the homogenization of American business. And it doesn't help a business like Church Street.

Independents are stifled by biased laws and outnumbered by corporate lawyers, but smart shops will find a way to take ideas from big businesses anyway. We can't (and shouldn't) take anything copyright protected, but we can adapt corporate ideas for our business models and our customers. At Church Street, we don't utter the word "frappuccino," but we do make a similar drink. And we use other ideas, like the way we handle a long line and the way we write on cups to be sure each detail of every drink gets communicated to the baristas. We don't take anything proprietary, of course, partly because we'd get sued, and partly because we think it's unethical. But we don't take our underdog status lying down. We fight back. And that's probably why we're still in business.

BRAVE NEW WORLD: NAVIGATING THE SMARTPHONE FRONTIER

Corporations don't just have corporate lawyers on their side; they have really big advertising budgets too. This advertising does more than just make us aware of companies and their products. It helps us know what to expect when we go into a big box store, and knowing what we'll find and how to act makes us more willing to go there. At Church Street, we didn't have a big budget of any kind, and we certainly didn't have any cash laying around to spend on advertising. So we used Facebook, Twitter and Instagram; not because we were such a cutting-edge shop that we needed a social media presence, but because it was free.

Cal's a bit of a Luddite. His favorite author and personal hero is Wendell Berry, a dude who sits on a farm writing about community. I think it's a safe bet to say Wendell Berry has never been on Instagram, which means that Cal doesn't want to be there either. For our first two years in business, Cal owned a flip phone. He thought LOL meant "lots of love." And he only uses Facebook to periodically ask his friends if he can borrow their kayaks. The point is, making sure Church Street Coffee & Books was relevant in the 21st century mostly fell to me.

Posting pictures of our books, our food and our drinks on social media was important because it let people know which products we offered, but it was using those tools to introduce our staff to customers that created the true magic. One of our biggest strengths at Church Street is that we prioritize friendliness, and that we really try to get to know people. Sharing photos of us having fun behind the counter was my way of inviting people to join in on that with us. So, I'd share a photo of Sri laughing and hashtag it "srilarious." I'd post the little gnome drawings and funny notes that Hoyt left behind the counter after his night shifts. And I'd put up pictures of Cal dancing, at least when he'd hold still long enough to let me get a decent shot.

Our staff were all very good sports about being on social media, but when I didn't feel like waving my iPhone in a staff member's face, I'd just take a selfie. I take a lot of selfies, and they're not all from Church Street. Seriously, probably half of the local beers and

coffee and local breakfasts that I buy end up on
the Internet. I know that makes me a bit of an online
joke — the girl with the Vespa and the hipster bangs who
Instagrams her scrambled eggs and vinyl record purchases. (Ha, lies! Hipsters don't eat scrambled eggs! Unless
they're made with prosciutto or sriracha or whatever the
new thing is that I haven't heard of yet but is cooler
than that stuff.) I've been accused of posting so much
because I'm obsessed with myself, but that's not why I
do it. I do it because it's been an incredibly successful
way of promoting my business, and because it helps me
promote other local businesses, too.

Because of social media, my best marketing tool was
my iPhone (whipped cream was also very useful — everyone wants to buy the Facebook drink when it's smothered
in whipped cream), and I pull my phone out pretty often
at the shop. But when I see a customer pulling out a
phone, it's another story. I get what Sri calls my "crazy
eyes" look, and that's because customers don't take
pictures of books to promote my shop on social media.
They take pictures of the books that I've chosen so they
can remember the titles and buy them more cheaply on
the Internet.

Taking product ideas from a brick-and-mortar store
and using them to search for discounted items online
is called "showrooming," and every physical store

from Best Buy to little ole Church Street deals with it. Grabbing a picture of a book I've searched out, read, reviewed, and displayed in my store so you can save five dollars by ordering it online is pretty rude, and using my research to fund Amazon, a company I believe is actively hurting books, makes me passionately upset. When I see someone showrooming, I usually want to shout or cry. Sometimes I want to throw hot coffee on that person's head. (I have a similar reaction when my friends use social media to promote corporately owned stores, or to post pictures of books they bought online instead of from me.)

I don't cry or yell or throw coffee because crying in front of your customers, or calling them stupid, or throwing scalding liquid at them, rarely gets you anywhere in business. (Okay, I haven't tried it, but I doubt it would work.) So I get that "crazy eyes" look because it's difficult to keep my mouth shut when a customer takes pictures of my books instead of buying them, or when they complain about the price of a book or a coffee. Once, a customer whined for so long about how expensive books are that Cal finally told him, "I'm using the money to feed my kids, if it makes you feel any better."

And that's the truth: When you buy local, you're feeding someone's kids. You're also making your streets safer and your schools better, and improving local government services. So if your kids go to public school and eat lunch there, you're kind of feeding your kids, too. Maybe that's reason enough to pull out your phone to tweet a positive shout-out for a local store instead of showrooming. It might cost a few more dollars, but it'll be much better for your community and your conscience ... and I know my blood pressure would appreciate it as well.

BOOKS WILL BREAK YOUR HEART

Most small business owners are in love with the products we sell, at least to some degree. Because starting a small business is a great way to experience a pressure cooker of stress, but not a very good way to make money (in the short run, anyway), most of us are in business at least partly because we actually care about what we do. I know that's true for me and Church Street.

I really enjoy coffee. I like drinking it, and I like serving it. It sounds silly, but making a customized drink correctly can be a real joy. In our hectic, crazy world, it's very fulfilling to be able to make something go right for my customers, even if that something is as small as cup of coffee. I like seeing a customer's face light up when they find out that I know what a flat white is and how to make it. Pouring a perfect cappuccino feels great, and making latte art is just really fun. The alchemy that happens when you and the other baristas are having a good time and are able to include the customers in that experience is such a good feeling, and it's why I'm in the coffee business. Plus, the perpetual student in me likes geeking out over coffee and knowing the difference between a marble mocha and a macchiato.

But it will come as a surprise to no one that my real love is books. I happen to be a book nerd, but the best thing about bookselling is being able to connect people who don't like books with the absolute magic that is reading. Being a book matchmaker is my real talent, and it's absolutely fantastic. My secret to being able to connect people with their book soulmates is really just to listen and to empathize with them and to think about the stories from their perspectives. (And you know what's taught me to be empathetic like that? You guessed it — books.)

When students come looking for their required reading, I take it as a challenge to help them find a book that's school-approved that they'll also actually enjoy. If I can help them have a good time doing an assignment they thought they'd dread, my mission is accomplished. (For some reason, non-readers often really like Vonnegut, and his books have been a gateway drug to further reading for a lot of my customers.) When I can help a customer discover a new author that an algorithm would never have chosen for them but that I know they'll truly connect with, my day is made. I get to learn customers' reading preferences, and sometimes I'm even able to save them from books they'll hate and, instead, recommend alternatives they'll really enjoy.

Our culture has moved pretty far away from reading anything that's longer than 140 characters, but in a way that's good for me, because it gives me lots of opportunities to change the minds of people who think they hate to read. The look in somebody's eyes when they come back raving about a book I talked them into buying is absolutely addictive. I know it's idealistic, but I really do believe that opening up the world of reading to someone is such a gift, because it's such a cheap and accessible way to travel, to learn about new things, and to be empowered to change your life or change the world. There's something about being totally immersed in a world of story, like you are when you read, that feels really good — even in a world of bite-sized information like ours. Watching people discover that feeling is amazing.

I love matching people up with books, but I also love being a professional book buyer. (The fact that "professional book buyer" is even a job title, let alone one that I have, still kind of blows my mind.) Choosing books for the shop is like going Christmas shopping every day, except that I'm shopping for my whole community. I love discovering new authors, finding gems that you wouldn't necessarily find in other stores, and searching for just the right book for one of my customers. It feels like a treasure hunt, and with books, there's always more treasure to find. Ordering titles, opening the box the next day and rediscovering the books I chose, and then making a book display is one of my favorite processes in the world. Even when I'm not actually in the store to help customers find what they want, my shelves speak for me, and they communicate my passion to others.

I sound like a fan girl when I talk about books, and that's because reading is crazy important to me. That's the reason I love my job, but it's also the reason it can be so tough. As much as I love connecting people with books, I don't get to do it as often as I'd like. Most of my time is spent, not talking about reading, but listening to people tell me why they don't have time to read. Busy people of the world, I have news for you: No one has time to read. Yep, it's true. There's always something easier or more urgent or more fun than reading. Those of us who do read don't do it because we have spare time. We do it because it's important and because reading helps us learn about the world outside ourselves. Yes, reading can be amazing, but in a culture like ours, it's something that we have to carve out time for: that we have to fight for. It doesn't just happen because we have carefree lives. (I've purposely put this rant near the end of the book so that everyone who reads this far can feel smug and superior. You're welcome!)

Reading is crazy important to me. That's why it upsets me when people don't make time to read. It's why it's offensive to hear people say that it isn't worth paying full price for books. It's why it bothers me so much when people buy from Amazon. (Most people think I hate Amazon because I'm a bookseller, but really the opposite is true — I'm a bookseller because I hated what Amazon was doing to books, so I opened a bookstore to do my part to stop it.) I care about what I sell, and that's part of why I take my business so personally. But, here's the secret about the owners of small shops: We all care about what we do. We all take it personally.

CONFESSIONS OF A PUNCHING BAG

Remember those Portlandia shopkeepers I mocked at the beginning of the book? The ones who couldn't stop complaining or correcting the customers and relied on pity to drive business? Well, now I know how they feel. Owning a shop (or working in customer service at all, really) can be like walking in an emotional minefield. It means fighting so hard to create something special, and then seeing that thing ignored or rejected on a daily basis. It can wear on you after awhile, and it's no wonder some shopkeepers turn to their cats for company: The shop cat is unlikely to complain that you made her cappuccino too dry.

Customers complain all day, sometimes about valid issues (if you got the wrong drink or you were treated badly, you have a perfect right to speak to management), and often about silly things (they dislike the other customers, they think the music is too loud, they want to borrow a pen and they're mad that you're out of pens because too many people borrowed them already). But personal snarkiness is nothing compared to what happens online. Church Street has been extraordinarily lucky, and most of our online reviews are positive. Apparently, cookies put people in a good mood and make them eager to share their happiness on Yelp, and I truly appreciate that.

But most of my other business-owning friends haven't been so fortunate, and their businesses have bad reviews I know they don't deserve because angry customers tend to leave reviews while satisfied customers don't. I know this hurts: I once saw a customer vaguely complain about Church Street's Christmas music on his Twitter feed, and it tore me up. I spent half the day crying, and he hadn't even used the name of the shop in his post. (It was our shop's first holiday retail season, I was an exhausted and emotional wreck, and this was a straw-that-broke-the-camel's-back kind of moment.) Social media is a helpful tool for complaining about big businesses, because there's no other way to be heard. With small shops, the attacks are usually just kinda mean.

Almost as bad as those people who Twitter-bash you or scream at you are the people who think they're helping. Opening a business is like wearing sandwich board reading, "Please critique my ideas and tell me how you'd do it better." For the first year or so, I was exhausted by people giving me ideas on how to grow my business: They want Church Street to be a chain. They want us to serve lunch. They want us to serve alcohol. They want us to start a book-of-the-month subscription service. The list goes on for what feels like forever.

I didn't take these ideas. It's not that I didn't want to grow my business; it's just that I knew I needed to create a strong foundation first. For the record, here's my reasoning: We shouldn't expand into a chain because new businesses go under when they try to over-reach quickly. I don't serve lunch because making sandwiches causes too much of a bottleneck in the coffee line. I don't serve alcohol because I don't know the bar business (and because I don't want to deal with you when you're drunk). And I don't do a subscription service because shipping makes already-expensive books too pricey.

But you probably don't want to hear my reasons, and neither did these well-intentioned customers. Coffee shops and bookshops are the stuff of dreams — lots of people imagine opening one someday. When people give me ideas, they're not trying to criticize my bookstore. They're just dreaming about having one of their own. When I finally figured that out, I chilled out a lot and I got better at listening instead of making excuses. I probably saved myself from becoming one of those awkward shopkeepers, too; which is good, because I'm allergic to cats.

Most of our customers are pretty awesome, and if they're rude it's more likely that they're having a thoughtless moment than purposely being unkind. It's best not to call people out on their behavior, but it can still be tough to hear the same insults day after day, even if they're accidental. For example, what am I supposed to say to the parents who tell me, "I *WISH* I had time to read like you, but I have kids." Should I tell them how much it hurts me that I don't have kids? Should I urge them to read more fiction in hopes that they'll be better at empathizing, learn to think before they speak, and consider that a single woman might not need to be repeatedly shamed for being childless? Yeah — probably not. That thoughtlessness is understandable, but it can also be tough to take. I'm not saying it's okay to be a Portlandia-style shopkeeper, but I do understand how people get there.

OWNING A BUSINESS: A LITTLE FUN, A LOT OF SHIT

Running the store was all the work I'd expected it to be. When people ask me what they should do to start a business, I tell them the first step is to learn to fix a toilet. What I don't tell them is they're going to have to fix that toilet while on the phone with a creditor, and a customer will somehow get past the lock and not understand why they can't just "real quick" use the toilet that's in pieces at your feet, and you'll have to smile and apologize profusely and ask them how their day's going while you're up to your elbows in someone else's shit. Running the shop was hard work, and a lot of toilet fixing, but I'd expected that. The weeks were spent standing up constantly, running from place to place (literally), putting out fires (sometimes literally, mostly metaphorically), carrying boxes full of cups (awkwardly large, but not heavy) and books (deceptively small, and very heavy), changing light bulbs (Again with the light bulbs!), and doing it all with a smile on my face so customers feel like they're in a happy place.

In some ways, of course, I really was in a happy place. The store was a success — we wouldn't be out of the woods financially for another three years, but even in the early days it seemed clear we wouldn't be one of those six-month start-ups. We tried to be welcoming, and it worked: It isn't unusual for our entire café to be engaged with each other in one big conversation. Neighbors run into each other and say hello every morning. High schoolers come in every afternoon and discuss exams and the stock market. (Yes, really, the stock market. I do not pretend to understand American teenagers.) It was exactly what I'd wanted, but I've never felt like I was a part of it. I'm the person (well, one of the persons) who keeps it running, and that means I'm always separate from the enjoyment of it, at least in part.

It's true that I personally care about all our staff members, but I'm not buddies with most of them. It's hard to be somebody's friend when you have to say, "Cool story, but could you stop telling it and stock the pastry case?" I realized pretty quickly that what our staff needed wasn't another friend — they had plenty of friends. They needed a boss, and that meant I wouldn't be invited out drinking, and I wouldn't be the person they shared their stories with. I'd be the person who sent them the schedule, even when they didn't like it. I'd be the person who reminded them that their breaks only lasted ten minutes, not twenty. It's good for people to be able to be mad at their bosses, sometimes justifiably and sometimes not as much. It's good to be able to test your limits against your boss without thinking you're going to hurt their feelings or alienate a friend. There's a difference between showing your staff that they matter to you and trying to be everybody's BFF. Too many independent shop owners try to be the latter, and it usually doesn't work out. I learned that pretty quickly, and I shaped up. It was good for the staff, and it was probably good for my personal growth. But it was hell on my social life; I never expected running the store to be so emotionally difficult.

Am I putting my heart on my sleeve? Yes, and that's the point — as shopkeepers, we put our hearts into independent shops. We're dealing with real human emotion instead of a corporate script, and while that can be beautiful, it can also be messy. I'd worked happily as a barista and bookseller before opening Church Street, but I didn't realize that what I'd loved about those jobs was the camaraderie I had with the rest of the staff. I thought, since Cal and I were working in the trenches with the baristas, making lattes and cleaning bathrooms and shelving books, the dynamic would be the same, but being a boss changed things more than I'd ever imagined.

I was very lucky to have a business partner who could understand how hard it is to run a business, but we barely saw each other in the first two years. Our business meetings happened in the alley over the ten minutes it took Cal to smoke a couple of cigarettes. He managed the store in the morning, I ran it in the afternoon and at night, and we didn't have time to commiserate. I was out of energy, out of patience, and out of personal money, since I barely took a salary from the store. (That $13,000 salary I mentioned earlier? That's all I took home from the store in the entire first year.) I was living off of apples, peanut butter sandwiches, granola bars and coffee for the first few months, which tanked my blood sugar. I felt lonely and isolated and unable to cope with stress at the time that I most needed to. I was barely holding it together, just hoping nobody rocked the boat.

CARRIE ROLLWAGEN

WHEN THE GOING GETS TOUGH, THE TOUGH GET HIGHER TAXES

Opening a small business is difficult even at the best of times, but the American system is now set up against small business interests, favoring only the very rich and powerful. Big business gets tax breaks while small businesses get hit with an uneven tax burden that's only compounded by audits. Big box stores are courted and embraced by communities willing to give them almost anything they ask for, while small shops are shackled with inflexible leases, zoning commission whims, and market changes — all while getting very little support from their local governments. Most of us think the playing field is even, but I've learned that it's more like one team is given a government-subsidized quarterback, free helmets and uniforms, a lifetime supply of Gatorade, pretty cheerleaders and a head start, while the other team is only allowed to play with half their players.

Entrepreneurship means being willing to compromise, raise support when you need it, and trust people (including staff and customers) to help you out. It's not something you can do alone, and leaning on other people often means getting let down. Running a business takes a willingness to push forward even when you're being attacked from every side — and you will be attacked from every side. Friends you'd thought would stand by you get jealous and try to take you down. People you ask for help will accuse you of taking advantage of them. You will read terrible things about yourself and your business on the Internet. The attacks will not be just about your business; they'll be about you. I was shocked that I lost personal relationships to my business, but I've since learned that my experience is shared by almost every entrepreneur that I know.

Almost every small business owner I know is worn out to the point of exhaustion most of the time. We're burdened with more taxes, more headaches and more community responsibility than the big stores, and we're cracking under the stress. Our health suffers. Our families suffer. Our friendships are tested and, many times, are broken. Entrepreneurship pulls apart people, marriages and families. Look at the children of business owners, and you won't find a single kid who didn't, at some point, feel that the business was more important. Look at our spouses, and you won't find one who doesn't sometimes feel alienated and sidelined. And for those of us who are single, that solitude that seemed manageable and even pleasant before the business opened starts to cut deep as the pressures of the shop become painfully isolating.

Locally owned stores are so good for our communities. They create jobs and great neighborhoods and an enjoyable life for all of us. They put more money into our local economies, and I think it makes sense to protect the people who create these shops instead of martyring them. Owning a shop or a business will never be easy, but it could be easier. If consumers supported local stores with money so that we as local shop owners had the time to actually care for ourselves and our relationships, that would help. If our stores weren't faced with a heavier tax burden than big box stores, we might be able to hire managers to reduce our stress levels. If the whole system weren't stacked against us, if it didn't seem like the weight of the world were on our shoulders, that might make carrying our own burdens a little bit easier.

After three years in business, I stopped working at Church Street and transitioned to silent partner. I wanted to work as a writer again and leaving was ultimately my decision, but breaking away from the store I'd built was extremely difficult anyway. I felt like I was being ripped away from my community. As it turns out, my community was stronger than that. When I finally ventured out of the hobbit-hole of my apartment and got back into the world after leaving Church Street, the small shops I'd been supporting with my money supported me right back with their kindness and generosity. I realized that I mattered to people, not just because I sold them books or made them coffee, but because they actually cared about who I was. I really believe it was small shops that kept me connected and (relatively) sane through one of the toughest transitions of my life.

IT WAS THE BEST OF TIMES

As difficult as running the shop sometimes was, I still had more good days than bad. I enjoyed my customers, I'm still obsessed with books, and I absolutely love my staff. I'm so proud that we built a place that really does foster community, and I'm amazingly thankful for everyone and every story that's been a part of ours. I love that Church Street sells books, and that we built a thriving bookstore in the age of the ebook. I'm thrilled that book groups meet at Church Street, and retired lawyers show up in the afternoons to discuss the events of the day, and that we sell picture books that today's children will remember forever. I love that there are kids in college now who've been buying books and cookies from me since they were in elementary school, and I'm proud that it's very likely they'll still be able to buy books from the shop I built when they're having their own children.

I've had my share of heartbreak at Church Street, but I've also had an amazing amount of success. Not everything worked out the way I'd planned, but what in life does? I think the fact that our story is messy makes it even more beautiful — that was true for Church Street, and it's true for other independent shops, too. Because we prioritize our employees, they're more likely to take pride in their work and to do interesting and important things in the future. Because we make unique buying decisions, we introduce diversity and pride of workmanship into the economy. And because we put so much money into our communities through taxes and charitable giving, we're essential to the strength of our cities and neighborhoods.

The way we as individuals work out localism in our own lives won't be perfect either. During Shop Small, I went cold turkey and only bought from local shops, but that won't be the answer for most of us. It isn't even the answer for me now: I'm still a localist, but I mostly buy local-ish. There are places I draw the line (I do my best never to shop at Wal-Mart or Amazon), but I do enjoy the occasional trip to Whole Foods. When we think about what we spend, it helps us think about the way we live. It helps us care more about each other and love each other better. We don't have to martyr ourselves or overhaul our spending habits completely to create more connection in

our lives and our communities; we just have to make a
few choices differently.

When I needed my community most, small shops
were there for me. They sold me breakfast and coffee
and beer, sure. But they also asked about my day, encouraged me in my writing, and donated money to make
this book happen. Even in an isolationist culture like
ours, even at one of the loneliest and scariest times in
my life, I wasn't alone. That's one thing small shops give
us that doesn't show up in statistics, but to me it was
the most important thing they could've done. Each of us
is connected to other people, and honoring that connection has changed the way I look at life. Shopping locally
is about more than just spending. It's about accepting
our responsibility to care for other people.

The reason I'm so passionate about shopping locally
isn't really that it puts money back into our communities.
I do think that's important, but frankly, economics just
doesn't motivate me enough to write a whole book about
it. What does motivate me is reminding people that they
matter, and that even in the face of globalized politics
and corporate greed, individual choices are meaningful. I
believe shopping small reminds us of that fact.

As individuals, as citizens, what we do and who
we are is significant. We have the power to change
the world, even with a seemingly small thing like our

spending. Each of us has the power to create something beautiful through our purchases. When we prioritize connection and community and each other, we're building something beautiful, not just with our spending, but with our lives.

READ MORE FROM THE LOCALIST

Read updates on the buy local movement and The Localist book at localistbook.com. Find more from Carrie Rollwagen at carrierollwagen.com, or on social media @crollwagen.

RESOURCES

Read the book Big Box Swindle by Stacy Mitchell

Visit the Institute for Local Self-Reliance at www.ilsr.org

Visit American Independent Business Alliance at www.amiba.net

Read the book Fast Food Nation by Eric Schlosser

Read the New Yorker article about Amazon — Cheap Words: Amazon is good for customers. But is it good for books? — by George Packer in the magazine's archives or online at newyorker.com.

Read the Salon article about Amazon — Worse than Wal-Mart: Amazon's sick brutality and secret history of ruthlessly intimidating workers — by Simon Head at salon.com.

Read the book Mindless: Why Smarter Machines Are Making Dumber Humans by Simon Head.

Read the blog Eating Alabama and find information about film screenings at eatingalabama.com.

Find a local bookstore with the free IndieBound App, or at www.bookweb.org

Find a local record store with the free App Vinyl District

The study that researched how much money from every $10 bill goes back into local economies studied 10 cities. It was performed by Civil Economics and was funded by the American Booksellers Association. Find more information on this study at www.amiba.net.

ACKNOWLEDGEMENTS

Creating *THE LOCALIST* story took a true community of people, and I'm so thankful to everyone who
helped make this book a reality. My editor, Bobby
Watson, helped me shape my ramblings and blog posts
into a cohesive narrative. His insights were unerring,
and he helped keep my vision and my voice intact while
making the book infinitely more readable. I'm continually amazed by the vision and talent of Andrew Thomson,
who's not only my book designer, but also a constant
source of creative inspiration. Jonathan Walls built a
website that makes it easy for readers to engage with
THE LOCALIST and with me, and he was always willing
to listen and to remind me that, even when times are
dark, there are friends, and there is Harry Potter.

I wrote most of this book on trains and in the homes
of Elisa Munoz and Zack Miller, and of Anna and Ross
Porter. They always had couches and beers waiting for
me, always supported me, fed me and made me laugh,
and reminded me of my vision when writing the book
got too tough. I love you all, and I don't think I couldn't
have survived this without you.

Kelly Cummings, Morgan Trinker and Carla Jean
Whitley served as my advisors, advocates and drinking buddies throughout this crazy adventure. I never

would've met them without my blog, Shop Small, and they constantly inspire me and kick my ass into gear with their business sense, their unwavering marketing genius, their humor and their champagne.

I'm grateful to my partners in crime and in business (well, mostly just business for me) who have come through for me over and over again: Seth Newell, who made my Kickstarter video and who I never tire of fighting with; John Yam, whose creative and financial advice is my secret weapon; David Carrigan, who double-checked my budget, assuaged my fears and fought with me about religion; Cary Norton, who came through yet again with author photos and moral support; and Kevin Wilder, who is always my best cheerleader in writing and in affairs of the heart.

To Jon Clemmensen, who saw the diamond in the very rough early drafts of *THE LOCALIST* and encouraged me to pursue the book; to Josh Miller, for making my writing sharper and coming through with support and with wit every time I needed you; to Abram Sheets, who not only listened to me vent but also walked me through print bleeds and color matching; to Sri Koduri, who knows when I need a cappuccino and when I need a whiskey; and to Jennifer Crabb, who has always believed in me and in my writing, and who will always be my kindred spirit — thank you.

THE LOCALIST was printed with the help of 179 Kickstarter backers who came through for me over and over again: most especially Kitty Rogers Brown, a fellow bulldog who's given me unwavering support ever since we opened Church Street, and Jason Lovoy, who kept my spirits up and kept me in copywriting work so I could actually make a living while writing a book.

I am forever thankful to all my blog readers, all my supporters, and to the local shopkeepers who inspired me and kept me in coffee and beer through my Shop Small year and beyond.

Thank you.